PRAISE FOR
THE PRESENTING BOOK

"How you present yourself to the world, communicate your ideas and differentiate yourself from others will ultimately determine your success in life. This book urges all of us to take inspiration from how big brands are managed and apply these branding techniques to 'brand you' so you can shine a spotlight on your key strengths and carve a niche that differentiates you from your peers."

Ivor Burns
Head of Marketing Strategy & Activation, Camelot

"Nicole Soames clearly shows that when it comes to presenting, less is generally more. This book is packed with practical steps to help you banish any nerves and deliver a confident and polished performance that captures and holds your audience's attention."

Jaana Tuominen
CEO, Fiskars Group

"Unlike most other books on presenting, *The Presenting Book* doesn't only focus on how to give big formal presentations. Instead, it reminds us that the secret to success is consistently presenting the best version of ourselves in every day, informal situations."

Ho-Yan Yap
Head of Recruitment and European Training and Development, Lazard

"I'm a big believer that you need to grasp every opportunity to differentiate yourself and stand out from the crowd. Nicole's practical, step-by-step approach will help you achieve this so that you make a great impression, whatever the situation."

Bruce Alexander
Managing Director, Montezuma's Chocolates

Published by
LID Publishing Limited
The Record Hall, Studio 304,
16-16a Baldwins Gardens,
London EC1N 7RJ, UK

info@lidpublishing.com
www.lidpublishing.com

A member of:

businesspublishersroundtable.com

© Nicole Soames, 2020
© LID Publishing Limited, 2020

Printed in Latvia by Jelgavas Tipogrāfija

ISBN: 978-1-912555-71-0

Cover design: Matthew Renaudin
Page design: Caroline Li

THE PRESENTING BOOK

PRACTICAL STEPS ON HOW TO
MAKE A GREAT IMPRESSION

NICOLE SOAMES

MADRID | MEXICO CITY | LONDON
NEW YORK | BUENOS AIRES
BOGOTA | SHANGHAI | NEW DELHI

FOR OTHER TITLES
IN THE SERIES...

CONCISE
ADVICE
LAB

SMALL BOOKS: BIG IDEAS

CLEVER CONTENT, DYNAMIC IDEAS, PRACTICAL
SOLUTIONS AND ENGAGING VISUALS –
A CATALYST TO INSPIRE NEW WAYS OF THINKING
AND PROBLEM-SOLVING IN A COMPLEX WORLD

conciseadvicelab.com

CONTENTS

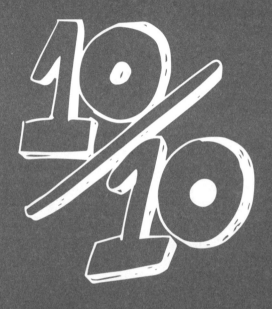

INTRODUCTION

1. MAKING A GREAT IMPRESSION

Given today's unprecedented levels of uncertainty and change, where everyone is bombarded with a non-stop flow of digital information, the ability to cut thorough the noise and make a memorable impression has never been more important. As you constantly compete for people's time and attention, how you present yourself to the world and communicate what you can bring to the table, either in person or virtually, is the key to standing out from the crowd.

First impressions really do count. Like it or not, human beings are hardwired to make snap judgements. The human brain instinctively categorizes people to help us make sense of the world. This unconscious bias can be based on appearance, age, gender, skin colour and social status, to name but a few. You, therefore, need to take active steps to manage this bias by controlling the 'controllables' – your tone of voice, body language and spoken word – in order to present your unique combination of skills, expertise and personality in the best possible light. After all, as the saying goes, you never get a second chance to make a great first impression.

Think about someone in your own life who has made a lasting impression on you – it could be a public figure, a friend, a client or a boss. Remember how they make you feel when you are with them. Do they inspire trust? Are they confident and credible? Do you enjoy spending time with them? Now think about how you can bottle this feeling. This is the gold dust that enables you to differentiate yourself from those around you. Don't fall into the trap of presuming these people are 'natural' presenters or 'born with' charisma. It takes hard work and commitment to present the best version of yourself. No one is the finished article. As with learning any new skill, there are practical steps you can take to put your best foot forward and present yourself clearly and confidently.

While it's crucial to make an impact when you first present yourself to someone, it's equally important to build credibility and trust over time by presenting yourself in a consistent manner. If, for example, the first time you meet a customer you go out of your way to make a connection and have a meaningful conversation, but in subsequent meetings you appear distracted and ill-prepared, your credibility is immediately eroded. Inconsistencies in behaviour can undermine trust as the other person will quickly conclude that you are not what you appear. Bear in mind these wise words from CEO Warren Buffet: "It takes 20 years to build a reputation and five minutes to ruin it. If you think about that, you'll do things differently."[1] Throughout this book, we will look at presentation best practice and apply this to the everyday, so that you can learn how to **do things differently** and present the best version of yourself each and every time you interact with someone.

2. PRESENTING YOURSELF FORMALLY AND INFORMALLY

In my experience, you are more likely to devote extra time and effort to how you present yourself when you are preparing for those big moments in your professional life such as a job interview, a pitch to a new client or giving a keynote speech at a conference. These are formal scenarios where the stakes are high and there is pressure to perform to the best of your ability. Where you generally let yourself down is in your informal, day-to-day life. I'm sure all of us are guilty at one time or another of putting less effort into how we come across in team meetings, at networking events, or via email or social media. Successful people, on the other hand, understand that they need to consciously make a great impression at every touchpoint they have with other people.

The secret is to flex your presenting style according to the particular situation you are in.

On the following page is a diagram that highlights the various formal and informal presenting situations people typically experience as part of their day-to-day lives:

FORMAL
- Presenting to team
- Speaking at a conference
- Customer meetings
- Performance appraisals
- Interviewing for a new job
- LinkedIn, company website
- Emails, Skype, phone calls

INFORMAL
- Attending a team meeting
- Networking at a conference
- Entertaining customers
- Socializing with team
- Facebook, Instagam, Twitter
- Emails, Skype, phone calls

As the diagram shows, there will be some overlap between the formal and the informal. For example, how you present yourself on social media will depend to a certain extent upon your audience. The impression you want to make on LinkedIn is likely to be more formal than the one you want to convey on Facebook or Instagram. However, you still need to present a consistent image that reflects the 'real professional you.' We have all heard of employers who have checked out the social media profiles of potential candidates as part of the recruitment process, only to find a discrepancy between the professional image they have presented in person versus the embarrassing holiday photos online.

Take a moment now to identify the situations where you feel you present yourself well, then focus on those areas you need to improve upon and jot them down in the table on the next page. It may be that you feel comfortable presenting to your team but struggle with stage fright when you present to a larger audience. Remember to be kind to yourself. Don't be a perfectionist; instead, try to be objective and concentrate on those areas you feel you need to develop.

EXERCISE

FORMAL SITUATIONS		INFORMAL SITUATIONS	
Do Well	Need to improve	Do Well	Need to improve
For example: Presenting to less than 20 people	Presenting to more than 10 people	For example: Socializing with my colleagues	Entertaining customers

3. DIALLING UP YOUR EQ TO PRESENT THE REAL YOU

Now that you have identified the presenting situations you want to work on, it's time to harness your emotional intelligence (EQ) to present yourself in a convincing and compelling way. In an age dominated by social media and a desire for perfection, it can feel risky to present the real you instead of an idealized version of yourself. In my opinion, many people mistakenly believe they need to fake it until they make it. However, pretending to be someone you are not is exhausting in the short, medium and long term. You can end up trying to be all things to all people and are likely to become unstuck at some point.

Another thing to remember is to not be tempted to copycat other people. While you can get inspiration from others, it is important to feel comfortable in your own skin and have the courage to express your genuine opinions and thoughts. Remember, successful people stay true to their core values and have the confidence to communicate their authentic selves.

EQ – **the ability to recognize and manage your own emotions and those of others** – holds the key to helping you identify the real you and communicate it effectively to your various audiences. (I use the term 'audience' throughout this book to refer to the receivers of your messages. These could be a customer, a colleague or a group of people.)

The diagram below breaks down EQ into three core areas. Let's examine each of these in turn to highlight the skills you need to develop in order to make a great impression.

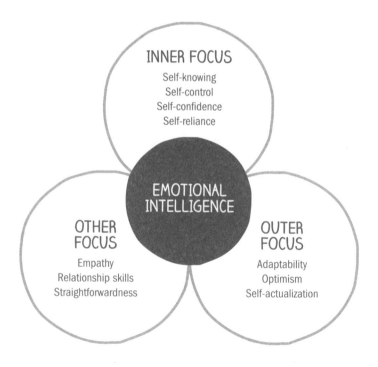

INNER FOCUS
Self-knowing
Self-control
Self-confidence
Self-reliance

EMOTIONAL
INTELLIGENCE

OTHER
FOCUS
Empathy
Relationship skills
Straightforwardness

OUTER
FOCUS
Adaptability
Optimism
Self-actualization

If you start by looking at the **Inner Focus** circle, you will see that self-knowing is top of the list of skills. Self-awareness is often described as the cornerstone of EQ. This is because you need to take the time to work out what you do well and what you need to work on in order to raise your presenting game. Developing self-knowledge can be easier said than done. If you ask for feedback on your presenting style, chances are most people's comments will either be vanilla or overly critical. So be brave, hold up a mirror and give yourself a full appraisal to understand what really makes you tick. This means accepting the real you and drawing on your self-confidence and self-reliance to back yourself and believe in what you stand for. The challenge is to communicate with authenticity while drawing on your self-control to be situationally appropriate. Dialling up your self-control will enable you to think and live in the moment, manage your stress levels and counter any nerves as you present. We will look at exactly how to do this in Part Six.

The skills in the **Other Focus** circle relate to your ability to leave a memorable impression on other people. You need to draw on your empathy to put yourself in your audience's shoes and understand their particular needs. By seeing things from their perspective, you can use your relationship skills to connect with them on a deeper level. This could involve having a meaningful conversation in an informal situation or asking rhetorical questions that capture your audience's attention in a more formal setting. Remember to be straightforward in your dealings with other people, as this will enhance your credibility and help you build trust over time.

As we move to the **Outer Focus** circle, you can see it contains those EQ skills that can help you to navigate different presenting situations. You need optimism to adopt a growth mindset and believe you can keep improving your presenting performance. By pushing yourself to move out of your comfort zone and into your stretch zone, you will achieve a greater sense of fulfilment and satisfaction for a job well done (self-actualization). Finally, adaptability plays a crucial role in your ability to present yourself in different ways depending on the particular situation you are in.

This should give you a quick overview of the powerful role EQ plays in honing your presenting skills, but don't worry if it feels like a lot to take in at first because we will look in greater detail at how to develop these skills later in this book.

4. HOW TO USE THIS BOOK

In my experience, most presenting books focus on the nuts and bolts of putting a presentation together instead of exploring presenting skills in a wider context. As a commercial skills trainer and coach with more than 25 years' commercial experience, my mission is to set you up for success by giving you the practical tools and techniques to unlock your EQ and present the best version of yourself, whether it's online or offline, informally or formally, to an audience of one or an audience of 500.

You need to be interested and interesting in order to make a genuine connection with the people to whom you are presenting yourself. This book will help you to achieve this by showing you how to develop your presenting confidence, build a powerful personal brand, understand the needs of your different audiences, capture people's attention and deliver your story with confidence so you are able to manage and control your messages.

I have designed this book to be used as a workbook, so don't be afraid to write notes in the margins and remember to complete the exercises! By committing to putting presenting theory into practice on a daily basis, you have taken the first very important step on your journey to becoming an inspirational presenter who creates a memorable impression on those around them.

PART ONE

CONFIDENCE

DEVELOPING YOUR PRESENTING CONFIDENCE

Confidence lies at the heart of making a good impression. It's not about being the loudest person in the room, it's about radiating self-assurance and self-belief. Confidence is contagious; you need to believe in yourself if you want to convince other people to believe in you too. For some people, confidence comes naturally but, for others, it can be harder to achieve. However, just like developing any skill, the more time and effort you put into building your confidence, the faster you will master it.

The first step to developing your presenting confidence is to recognize that confidence comes from within: you can't build it without taking action. People generally spend a lot of time *physically* preparing for presentations – whether it's writing a speech or putting PowerPoint slides together – but underestimate the *mental* preparation that is needed to make a good and lasting impression. This part of the book will give you the tools and techniques you need to get your head in the right place for *every* presenting situation. To quote the famous phrase: "Believe you can and you're halfway there."

1. KNOWING YOURSELF

Let's start by referring back to the EQ diagram on page 8. You will need to draw on the skills in the Inner Focus circle in order to develop your presenting confidence. Self-knowledge is crucial. You need to have your finger on your pulse so you can understand your feelings in different presenting situations. Look at the table of presenting situations you identified on page 6 that make you feel uncomfortable or insecure. Then, try to understand exactly *why* you aren't confident in a particular situation so you can take practical steps to work on building your confidence. This can be easier said than done as it can be difficult to define your emotions. A good technique is to ask yourself how you *feel* about the situation, rather than what you *think* about it.

It's helpful to break down your awareness into three key areas: emotional awareness (how you feel), behavioural awareness (how you impact others) and non-verbal communication (what your body language communicates to other people). As a rule, people generally have a heightened awareness of all three areas during formal presenting situations. For example, if you are going to a job interview, you are likely to ready yourself and calm your nerves (emotional awareness), speak confidently and clearly (behavioural awareness), and make sure to have a firm handshake and make regular eye contact (non-verbal communication). However, when was the last time you consciously focused on your hand gestures and tone of voice during a team meeting or networking event?

Understanding the impact you have on others and what your body language communicates about yourself can be difficult. All too often, we focus almost all of our attention on our spoken words, as the diagram below illustrates.

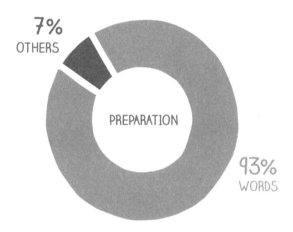

In fact, according to Albert Mehrabian's 7-38-55% rule, only 7% of what you communicate comes from your spoken words, while 93% of your impact comes from your tone of voice and body language.[2]

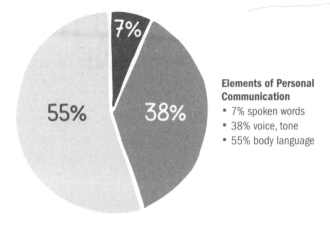

Elements of Personal Communication
- 7% spoken words
- 38% voice, tone
- 55% body language

Dr Albert Mehrabian's 7-38-55% rule

You therefore need to ask for feedback from others so you can develop a more balanced awareness of your communication style. Bear in mind that if you are the sort of person who is very animated and wears their heart on their sleeve, your non-verbal communication will be easier to read, whereas if you are more reserved and private, it can be more of a challenge for people to give feedback. By taking practical steps to increase your awareness of your emotional, behavioural and non-verbal communication, you will become ready to set goals to develop your presenting confidence and make a lasting impression.

2. MOVING INTO THE STRETCH ZONE

Now that you have an understanding of how to increase your awareness of how you feel and behave in different presenting situations, you need to harness your self-reliance and self-control to back yourself and move into your stretch zone. Moving out of your comfort zone can seem daunting at first – it's called a comfort zone for a reason, because it's the mental place where we feel emotionally secure. However, it's only by testing your limits that you can gain a clear understanding of what you are truly capable of.

I'm a big believer in the idea that 'what doesn't challenge us doesn't change us'. The graph on the next page highlights the important role challenge plays in developing your presenting performance.

PERFORMANCE

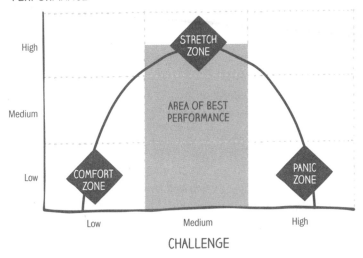

If you look at the bell curve through a presenting lens, you can see that the vertical axis shows an individual's performance levels and the horizontal axis reflects how challenged they are feeling. The graph clearly shows that, to develop your presenting confidence, you need to experience a medium level of challenge so as to move into your stretch zone – your area of best performance. As a rule, you are more likely to stay in your comfort zone when you are in more informal presenting situations. This could be due to complacency, boredom or even a lower priority being placed on making the most of new presenting opportunities. Formal presenting opportunities, on the other hand, are more likely to tip you into your panic zone, where once again performance levels will dip. This could generate feelings of being out of your depth, causing you to shy away from going the extra mile. Below are the signs to watch out for that will tell you you're in your presentation panic zone:

- You feel overwhelmed and can't think straight
- You find it difficult to make a decision on the presentation content
- You can't sleep properly or wake up worrying
- You suffer from tension headaches or stomach troubles in the run-up to the situation
- You dread any feedback on your presentation, even if it's constructive, as it feels like personal criticism

You have to have an appropriate level of challenge to be in your area of best performance so you can present with confidence. For some of you, this will be about stretch and trying something you've never tried before, while for others, it will be about being supported to get out of your panic zone and back into your stretch zone. Following are five steps to help you move into your presenting stretch zone:

1. **FACE YOUR FEARS.** Write a list of your main concerns, such as "they're going to judge my performance", and then think of a counterargument, such as "it gives me an opportunity to demonstrate my knowledge". By silencing your self-doubt in this way and reminding yourself that you are the subject matter expert, you will feel motivated to move into your stretch zone

2. **MAKE A PLAN.** Break down your goal into manageable chunks and draw up a plan of action. Remember you don't need to do it all in one go. Instead of agreeing to be a keynote speaker at a conference, develop your confidence by committing to hosting a webinar or speaking on a panel

3. **FIND SUPPORT.** Find a mentor, coach or colleague to help you develop your presenting confidence. They can give you feedback and help you calm your nerves (but more about this in Part Six)

4. **VISUALIZE SUCCESS.** Athletes use visualization techniques to help them achieve their peak performance. So, picture yourself making a great impression at the next team meeting or signing the contract for your new job

5. **BE INSPIRED BY OTHERS.** Who do you know who is a great presenter? Ask yourself what they would do in this situation

Complete the table in the next exercise to help you move into your area of best performance by setting yourself achievable goals within the next 12 months. Remember to fix your goals in time and place and identify a trusted friend, coach or colleague who can support you and hold you to account.

EXERCISE

PRESENTATION SITUATION GOAL	WHEN	WHO WILL HOLD ME TO ACCOUNT?
What will I start/ stop/continue?	When will I start/ stop/continue?	Who needs to be involved, provide me with feedback or hold me to account
For example: *Whole-company briefing – I will deliver a ten-minute presentation highlighting my team's purpose and go-to market strategy*	For example: *Within the next quarter*	For example: *My team, my boss, my coach*
(SPACE FOR ANSWER)	(SPACE FOR ANSWER)	(SPACE FOR ANSWER)

3. MANAGING EMOTIONAL INTERFERENCE

In order to achieve your presenting goals, you need to dial up your self-awareness to identify any limiting beliefs and then use your self-control to manage your response to them. Timothy Gallwey highlights this in his book *The Inner Game of Work* when he explains that interference creates noise which reduces our potential to perform.[3] In other words, to build your presenting confidence, you need to reduce those emotional concerns and worries that interfere with your ability to make a great impression.

The chart below outlines the different levels of interference that may affect you when you present:

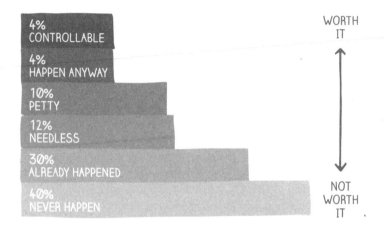

Let's start from the bottom and move upward. As you can see, a staggering 40% of what we worry about are hypothetical events that never actually happen, such as whether people will remember to turn up for our presentation, while 30% of our worries (or interference) are about things in the past that have already happened and can't be changed. This could be the challenging questions you had at the end of your last presentation. Needless worry accounts for 12% of our worries; examples could be dropping your microphone or having a coughing fit. Another 10% of our worries are about petty things such as questioning the choice of font on our presentation slides, and 4% of our worries are going to happen anyway (e.g. a colleague objecting to something you say in your team meeting) so there is nothing we can do to prevent them. Finally, only 4% of everything we worry about involves things that we can actually control – this could be what you say and how you say it.

The secret to moving into your stretch zone is to harness your self-control to banish the majority of these worries and focus instead on controlling the controllables. As is the case for many things in life, this is easy to say in theory but often hard to do in practice. As humans we have a tendency to think more about the negatives than the positives, which leads me nicely on to the important role optimism plays in developing your presenting confidence.

4. FEEDING THE GOOD WOLF

A useful analogy that illustrates the power of optimism is the story of the Two Wolves created by Billy Graham.[4] The tale begins with a grandfather telling his grandson, "There is a battle between two wolves that live inside us all. One wolf is evil and embodies anger, jealousy, regret, self-pity and guilt. The other wolf is good and represents peace, hope, benevolence, empathy and generosity." The grandson thinks about this for a while and asks, "Which wolf wins?" The grandfather replies, "The one you feed."

As this story highlights, you have a range of emotions that do battle within your head. However, by drawing on your optimism and looking for the positives in your presenting situation, you can actively choose to feed the good wolf and silence your negative thoughts so you can achieve your full potential.

Let's use the scenario of a job promotion to explore this idea in greater detail. Your bad wolf could be telling you, "It's not even worth putting myself forward for promotion as I'll never get it." By feeding the bad wolf in this way, you would shy away from the opportunity to present yourself in the best light. If, on the other hand, you fed the good wolf by deliberately thinking the direct opposite and concentrating on the positives of the situation, you could go into the interview believing, "I have a wealth of commercial and management experience that makes me highly suitable for the new role."

Unfortunately, silencing your bad wolf can be hard to do as our negative beliefs can be deeply entrenched. We are often our own harshest critics, so give yourself a break from time to time. A great way to do this is to imagine how a good friend who is on your side and accepts all your strengths and weaknesses would describe you. You then need to reinforce this positive thinking by finding evidence to support your new belief.

NEW BELIEF:
- I can sell myself effectively at interview

EVIDENCE:
- I articulate presentations well
- I have relevant skills, experience and expertise
- I have positive feedback from my team that supports my application

Complete the table in the next exercise to help develop your optimism and boost your presenting confidence for both formal and informal situations. The key is to start with the macro (large scale) and move to the micro (small scale): identify why you should feel confident about the presenting situation you are in, your relationship with the person or people you are presenting to, and yourself on a personal level.

EXERCISE

SPECIFIC DETAILS	WHY I SHOULD FEEL CONFIDENT
This situation ▶	
With this person/group ▶	
Me personally ▶	

By drawing on your optimism in this way, you are more likely to be solution-orientated and resilient. This means you will be able to bounce back from setbacks by taking what you have learned and moving forward. In the case of the promotion scenario, an optimistic person who didn't secure the new role would evaluate their performance and identify what went well and what needed to be improved upon so they could be better prepared for the next opportunity. By constantly raising the bar in this way, you will reap the rewards of increased presenting confidence and performance.

Finally, when it comes to developing your presenting confidence, practice really does make perfect. The key is being honest with yourself; no matter how experienced a presenter you are, there will always be scenarios where you feel panicked. It's how you manage this emotion that sets you apart from your peers. A powerful strategy to help you do this is to model yourself on someone who excels at presenting. It could be Steve Jobs, Michelle Obama or a colleague or friend; ask yourself how they prepare mentally so they can present the best version of themselves. After all, as I said in the introduction, none of us are the finished article – we need to follow these practical steps to get our head in the right place so we can continuously improve and be the very best that we can be.

KEY TAKEAWAYS

We've covered quite a lot of ground in this part of the book, so here's a quick reminder of the key steps you need to take to develop your presenting confidence:

- Confidence comes from within; harness your EQ skills to develop your self-belief and present the best version of yourself
- Dial up your self-knowledge to understand how you feel in different presenting situations
- Break down your self-knowledge into emotional awareness, behavioural awareness and non-verbal communication
- Only 7% of what you communicate comes from your spoken words, so adopt a more balanced awareness of your communication style
- Draw on your self-reliance and self-control to move into your stretch zone – your presenting area of best performance
- Experience a medium level of challenge to move into your stretch zone: too little and you stay in your comfort zone, too much and you tip into your panic zone
- You are more likely to stay in your comfort zone in informal presenting situations and your panic zone when you are faced with more formal presenting situations
- Face your fears and draw up an action plan, setting manageable goals to help you develop your presenting confidence
- Fix your presenting goals in time and place and identify someone who can support you and hold you to account
- Minimize any emotional interference that prevents you from reaching your presenting potential by concentrating your time and attention on those things you can control

- Feed your good wolf by silencing any negative thoughts and focusing on the positives of each presenting situation
- Reinforce positive thinking by finding evidence to support your new belief
- Develop a positive mindset by reminding yourself why you should feel confident about the presenting situation you are in, the people you are presenting to and yourself on a personal level
- Be inspired by those around you to keep raising your presenting game

PART TWO

BRAND
you

BUILDING A COMPELLING PERSONAL BRAND

Now that you have a better understanding of who you are and what makes you tick, you need to be able to communicate it effectively in order to build a strong personal brand. As Jeff Bezos, founder of Amazon, is famously credited with saying, "Your brand is what people say about you when you're not in the room." This doesn't mean you need to constantly worry about how you are being judged or try to be all things to all people. It's about making a conscious decision about what you want to be known for and being clear on the value you bring, not just what your job title tells people you do. Gone are the days when you could sit back and wait for praise for a job well done. In today's fast-paced world, you need to take practical steps to raise your profile so that you can stand out from the competition.

The secret to building a compelling personal brand is to carve out a niche and shine a spotlight on your strengths so you can land your key messages and make a memorable impression. By proactively taking control of your messaging and presenting the real you, you can attract like-minded people, who will be more likely to listen and trust you. After all, we all like doing business with people that are like we are.

A powerful example of this is the way in which Bill Gates has built his personal brand based on his intelligence, innovation and philanthropy. As a result of this authenticity, people have bought into his pledge to help make the world a better place through the Bill and Melinda Gates Foundation, thereby cementing his reputation as a globally trusted and respected thought leader. This was particularly evident during the early months of the coronavirus crisis, when he became a key spokesperson for rational thought and science. When you trust a brand in this way, you are proud to be associated with it. This is what you are trying to achieve person-ally. If you learn from the big brands, apply branding techniques on a personal level and present the real you, people will be able to connect with you emotionally, which will in turn help you to gain a greater sense of meaning and fulfilment. After all, according to Maslow's Hierarchy of Needs, you need a sense of belonging in order to be able reach your full potential.[5]

1. CREATING A STRONG FIRST IMPRESSION

I have already touched upon the importance of making a great first impression in the introduction; however, I want to examine this point in further detail, now, in the context of building your personal brand. A powerful way to bring this to life is to use the scenario of a job interview, where first impressions are particularly crucial to success. According to a study done by Princeton psychologists Janine Willis and Alexander Todorov,[6] it takes a mere seven seconds for people to make a judgement and form an impression of you. In this short time, the other person, often subconsciously, forms an opinion about you based on your appearance – from your demeanour to your mannerisms, and even how you are dressed. This first impression is nigh on impossible to reverse or undo, making those first encounters extremely important as they can set the tone for the relationships that are to follow.

There is no denying that creating a strong personal brand can open doors. Almost everybody now has a digital footprint, so before you even step foot in the interview, make sure you have audited yourself online to establish what is already out there about you.

You then need to focus on what I describe as the ABC of first impressions: your appearance, body language and communication.

First things first, you need to be punctual. If you turn up late to an interview, you will immediately create a negative impression. Allow plenty of time to get to the meeting so you appear cool, calm and collected rather than rushed and flustered. When you are faced with formal presenting situations, it can be easy to go into 'robot mode,' where you are so concerned about what you are saying that you lose some of your individuality. Remember, do not sign over your personality at reception when you get your visitor's badge. From the moment you walk through the door, you need to engage with everyone in an appropriately enthusiastic and approachable manner. This doesn't mean you need to fake it or be someone you're not – employers are likely to see through disingenuity; it's about presenting yourself in an authentic and credible way.

As humans we are hardwired to make snap judgements based on our unconscious biases, so take steps to control this by managing your appearance. You need to dress the part – but this doesn't mean going out and spending a fortune on a new wardrobe of clothes. It's about wearing clothes that fit you well and are situationally appropriate. Do your homework beforehand and find out the dress code of the company to which you are applying. You don't want to turn up in a suit and tie if you are applying for a creative role in an advertising agency. However, if you are unsure, I always recommend erring on the side of caution and going smarter rather than risk being underdressed. Your aim is to present a professional image that communicates and is in harmony with your brand. Think about the type of pen you are going to use – don't just grab the nearest chewed biro. If you have brought some documents to show them, make sure they are close to hand: you don't want to have to root around for them in your bag as it could suggest you are disorganized or nervous. Make sure your CV is printed out on high-quality paper, is easily digestible and articulates why you stand out from the competition. All of this may sound obvious, but you'd be amazed how many people underestimate the importance of managing these details.

The next step is to focus on your body language. You need to walk the talk. If you don't appear confident, you will be hard pressed to convince your potential employer that you are up to the job. Let's start with the introduction. You need to smile – this is the logo for 'brand you' – and make confident eye contact. Remember from Part One, over 55% of what you communicate comes from non-verbal cues. Your interactive style and the ebb and flow of the conversation will determine how confident you appear to the interviewer, as will any physiological responses such as clammy palms or flushed cheeks. Prepare ahead by anticipating any of these responses, so you can manage them. An example could be asking for a glass of water in case your mouth feels dry.

Now for the communication itself. Your opening lines need to position you as an expert in your field and the right candidate for the job. If you think about branding principles, these are about articulating the benefit of your personal brand in a succinct and confident manner. For example, whenever I introduce myself to someone for the first time, I say, "My name is Nicole Soames, and I'm on a mission to set people up for success by helping them become commercial athletes." Make sure you have rehearsed your personal brand statement beforehand, so there is no hesitation. Your overriding aim should be to use your personal brand to help you find common ground and make a genuine connection with the person interviewing you. Throughout the interview, you need to focus on what you say and how you say it – there is more about this in Part Four, where I focus on exactly how to deliver your key messages with confidence. Finally, after your interview, always send a follow-up email thanking the interviewer for their time and expressing your continued interest in the role and why you believe you are the right person for the job.

2. BUILDING TRUST AND CREDIBILITY

Gaining the trust of your target audience lies at the heart of building a powerful brand. Building trust means delivering on your promises and transforming people into advocates who recommend your company's products and services. Take Google, for example. Recent research in the US shows that people trust Google more than their own government.[7] Since 2008, Google has consistently established trust with its users by accurately helping people to navigate digitally via Chrome and physically via Google Maps. This is in sharp contrast to Facebook, where trust levels have declined rapidly as a result of the revelation that Cambridge Analytica inappropriately acquired the data of tens of millions of Facebook users.[8] As this example shows, to build credibility and trust you need to practise what you preach and behave in an honest and responsible way. These are principles that hold equally true when it comes to building your personal brand.

I often describe a personal brand as a secret weapon that helps you to establish your credentials and create value in the minds of your target audience. Zig Ziglar highlighted this when he said, "If people like you they will listen to you, but if they trust you, they will do business with you."[9] So, how do you put the building blocks in place to build this trust? In his bestselling book *The Speed of Trust*, Stephen Covey breaks down trust into the four core areas: integrity, intent, capabilities and results.[10]

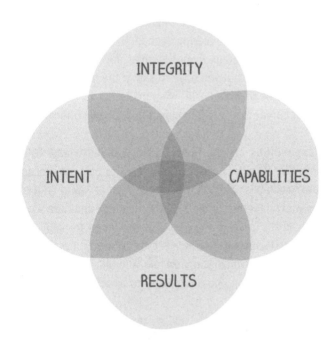

The first two areas, integrity and intent, relate to character, while capabilities and results are linked competence. Let's start by exploring the important role **integrity** plays in building trust. All too often people confuse integrity with honesty, when in fact it is more than this. Integrity is about behaving in a way that is true to your inner thoughts and values. It's about standing up for what you believe in and having the courage to do the right thing.

In the job interview scenario, this could be about ensuring that the culture of the company you are applying to aligns with your own personal values. The second core area to focus on is your **intent** – in other words, your personal agenda or motivation. If people doubt your motives, they are unlikely to trust you. Trust grows when people are honest and open about their intentions. If people think you have a hidden agenda, they are likely to be wary and suspicious, whereas if your motives are mutually beneficial, they will buy into what you have to say. In the interview situation, an example of this would be demonstrating to the interviewer how their company's values connect to your own principles.

Your **capabilities** are the talent, skills, knowledge and style you possess that inspire confidence. You need to be seen as capable in order to establish credibility and trust. A great way to do this is to play to your strengths, adopt a growth mentality and have a can-do attitude. In the case of the interview, you need to highlight your expertise and specialist knowledge to show that you will be able to hit the ground running in your new role. After all, if you fail to inspire confidence in person, you are unlikely to be offered the job.

The final area that builds trust is **results**. This is your performance together with your track record of success. There's no doubt that results matter – they signal to other people that you are an achiever who can be trusted to deliver. So, take responsibility for your results and remember to communicate them to other people. This is vital in an interview. Don't be afraid to blow your own trumpet; you need to be proud of your performance and what you have achieved. Take care with the language you use to describe your achievement, ensuring you use 'I' when it is genuinely appropriate.

EXERCISE

Complete the table below by finding examples of your integrity, intent, capabilities and results.

INTEGRITY (inner values and beliefs)	For example: *Coaching people in your team so they can reach their full potential* *(SPACE FOR ANSWER)*
INTENT (your motives/agenda)	For example: *To become a thought leader in my field* *(SPACE FOR ANSWER)*
CAPABILITIES (skills, expertise, knowledge)	For example: *Subject matter expert* *(SPACE FOR ANSWER)*
RESULTS (achievements, track record)	For example: *Keynote speaker, published author* *(SPACE FOR ANSWER)*

By focusing on developing these four core areas of credibility, you will be well on your way to creating a personal brand that inspires trust. The key is to remember to present your authentic self. Don't be frightened to show vulnerability – it will make you appear more human and believable. Richard Branson outlined the importance of authenticity when he said, "Too many companies want their brands to reflect some idealized, perfected image of themselves. As a consequence, their brands acquire no texture, no character and no public trust."

3. BEHAVING AND COMMUNICATING CONSISTENTLY

Brilliant brands behave consistently – you trust them because they deliver their brand promise in a consistent manner through all their stakeholder touchpoints. Apple is a great example of this. From its website design to its packaging and in-store experience, it displays simple, clean lines with white backgrounds that make its innovative products the centre of attention. This ensures that its consumers have a consistent experience, whether they are opening their new phone or talking to an Apple technician at the 'Genius Bar.' It's important to apply this consistency to your personal brand. On the following page are examples of the different touchpoints that your brand might have.

SOCIAL MEDIA

PHONE CALLS

FORMAL CONVERSATIONS

EMAILS

ONE-TO-ONES

MEETINGS

INFORMAL CONVERSATIONS

WEBINARS

EXERCISE

Rate yourself out of ten according to how consistently you communicate your brand in each of your touchpoints so you can identify specific areas to focus and work on.

It's essential that you guard against inconsistency (saying one thing and doing another), as this will cast doubt on your values and undermine your brand. As an EQ practitioner and coach who is passionate about helping people to improve their performance, I need to ensure this passion and commitment are evident in every email, phone call and conversation I have. It would seem disingenuous if I were indifferent in informal conversations and only saved my enthusiasm for formal presentations. The same consistency is needed when you start a new job. You need to carry on behaving as you did in your interview or your employer could think you were putting on an act to land the new role. This could undermine trust in the long run and leave them feeling duped. Once trust has been lost, it is extremely hard to rebuild.

EXERCISE

Now it's your turn to articulate your personal brand. Using all the knowledge you have gathered about yourself so far, fill in the Personal Branding Shield below to help you identify how to present your personal brand in an authentic and consistent manner. Try to summarize your personal brand into a simple two sentence statement that you can use to introduce yourself and make a great first impression. A great example is Richard Branson's personal statement: "Tie-loathing adventurer, philanthropist and troublemaker, who believes in turning ideas into reality. Otherwise known as Dr. Yes at @virgin!"

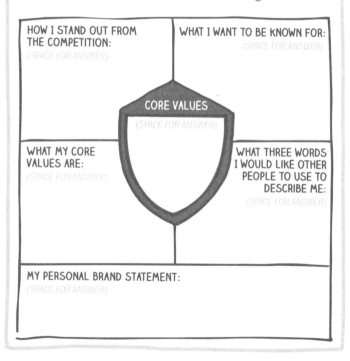

HOW I STAND OUT FROM THE COMPETITION:
(SPACE FOR ANSWER)

WHAT I WANT TO BE KNOWN FOR:
(SPACE FOR ANSWER)

CORE VALUES
(SPACE FOR ANSWER)

WHAT MY CORE VALUES ARE:
(SPACE FOR ANSWER)

WHAT THREE WORDS I WOULD LIKE OTHER PEOPLE TO USE TO DESCRIBE ME:
(SPACE FOR ANSWER)

MY PERSONAL BRAND STATEMENT:
(SPACE FOR ANSWER)

Finally, it's important to recognize that you can't build your personal brand in a day – it takes time to perfect and will evolve as you develop as an individual throughout your career. You need to constantly refine and polish your personal brand in order to build trust and credibility. Even Oprah Winfrey began by going through several style iterations on a small local show before defining her presentational style into one of the most influential personal brands in the world.

KEY TAKEAWAYS

You should now have a clear understanding of the powerful role your personal brand plays in making a great impression and winning the hearts and minds of your audience. Here's a quick recap of the main points:

- Actively build a compelling personal brand so you can raise your profile and stand out from the competition
- Shine a spotlight on your strengths so you can carve out a niche and differentiate yourself from your peers
- Take inspiration from the big brands, such as Apple and Google, and apply branding techniques to 'brand you'
- First impressions really do count – it takes a mere seven seconds for people to make a judgement about you
- A strong personal brand can open doors and help you to make a great first impression
- Focus on the ABC of first impressions – your appearance, body language and communication
- Around 55% of your communication comes from non-verbal cues, so make sure you dress the part and walk the talk
- Articulate your personal brand statement convincingly and confidently to make a great first impression
- Gaining trust lies at the heart of personal branding – to build trust, you need to behave in an honest, consistent and responsible way
- Use Stephen Covey's four core areas of credibility (integrity, intent, capabilities and results) to help you build trust with your target audience

- Brilliant brands behave consistently by delivering on their brand promise via every touchpoint
- Take a leaf out of Apple's book and ensure you keep your communications consistent through each of your touchpoints – both informally and formally
- Use the Personal Branding Shield to help you identify what you want to be known for – make sure this incorporates your key values as well as the skills that make you stand out from the competition
- Take the time to craft your personal brand statement – it needs to be succinct (no more than a couple of sentences), articulating the value you bring and why you stand out from the crowd
- Remember that your personal brand will evolve over time as you grow and develop as an individual – you need to constantly refine and polish it so that it reflects your authentic self

PART THREE

SETTING YOURSELF UP FOR SUCCESS

Once you have recognized the power of a consistent, authentic and trustworthy personal brand, you need to take practical steps to set yourself up for success in specific presenting situations, whether formally or informally. I'm a big believer that if you fail to plan, you plan to fail. This means doing your homework for each and every presenting opportunity.

As a rule, you are more likely to prepare for formal situations, propelled by the feeling of being under pressure to perform well. Where it's easy to get caught off guard are those informal situations such as a webinar or video conference where you are more likely to feel confident enough just to wing it. I'm sure you can think of examples, especially if you were working at home during the coronavirus crisis, where you have been interrupted on a call by children, dogs barking or the doorbell ringing, creating a less-than-ideal impression. So, in this part of the book I'm going to set you up for success by helping you to understand the purpose of the presenting situation, showing you how to clarify the needs of your audience and match these with your own personal goals, and encouraging you to manage the environment in which you are presenting. Remember, when I use the term 'audience' it can refer to one person or a group of people depending on the presenting situation with which you are faced.

1. UNDERSTANDING THE PURPOSE OF THE PRESENTING SITUATION

The secret to understanding the real purpose of the presenting situation is to start with the end in mind. In other words, you need to ask yourself, "What is the outcome I want from this situation?" For example, if you are presenting your plans for the year ahead to your team, the purpose of the situation is to engage them and get their buy-in, so they are excited and energized and ready to hit the decks running. If you are representing your department at a company update meeting at the town hall, the purpose could be to put your team on the map, establish your credentials and demonstrate the values you bring collectively. Turning to an informal example, such as a first video call with a new member of your team, the outcome you want to achieve is to help them understand who you are and how they can build a relationship with you.

A great tool to help you work out the purpose of each situation is the Think, Feel, Do model.

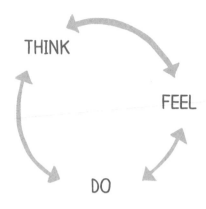

THINK

FEEL

DO

Before each presenting situation, you need to draw on your empathy to work out what your audience is currently **thinking**, how they are **feeling** and what they are **doing**. The next step is to identify what you would like them to think, feel and do as a result of your presentation. This will help you to understand how to introduce your key messages so you can achieve your desired end.

It's crucial that you know the direction you are heading in and what you want to achieve *before* you put the content of your presentation together. This will stop you going off track and save you precious time in the long run. It will also boost your confidence, enabling you to make a more meaningful connection with your audience. The secret to success is giving yourself the headspace to think things through so you can clarify the end result you desire. The time you take to do this will obviously depend on the nature of the presenting situation. You will need to devote more time to a company-wide presentation than you would to a video call with a member of your team.

Overall, by drawing on your empathy in this way to understand your audience's mindset, you will demonstrate that you are a person to be trusted rather than someone who is only focused on their own agenda.

Let's now apply the Think, Feel, Do model to one of the scenarios above to see exactly how you can understand and influence your audience's mindset. Imagine you are about to present your yearly plan to your team. Below are some examples of what their current mindset could be, together with examples of the desired outcome you might want to achieve from your presentation.

AUDIENCE MINDSET			
	THINK	FEEL	DO
CURRENT	Thinking of the list of pressing tasks they need to get through on a day-to-day basis	Feeling demotivated and overwhelmed by their workload	Focused on the short term, relying on themselves to deliver the results
DESIRED	Thinking about the bigger picture and ensuring they consider short-term tasks in the context of the longer term	Feeling excited to be part of a wider team that collaborates and supports one another	Communicating in advance, working with others to find solutions and think creatively

By preparing this ahead of your team meeting, you can start thinking of the key messages you want to convey as part of your presentation, such as:

- The team is bigger than the sum of your individual contributions
- Rather than operating in silos, you will benefit from collaborating with others
- Adopting a more joined-up and strategic way of working will be energizing
- Your goal is to be a creative thinker who can communicate and collaborate effectively while keeping your sight on the longer term

EXERCISE

Now it's your turn. Use the exercise below to help you prepare for a specific presenting situation you have coming up. Remember to use your empathy and awareness to understand how your audience is feeling in the here and now as well as what you want them to think, feel and do after you have presented.

	AUDIENCE MINDSET		
	THINK	FEEL	DO
CURRENT			
DESIRED			

2. CLARIFYING THE NEEDS OF YOUR AUDIENCE

In addition to understanding your audience's mindset, you need to clarify their needs by using your emotional intelligence (EQ) to ask clever questions and actively listen to their responses. For example, if you are representing your department at a town hall – a more formal scenario – you should take active steps to tap into the needs of your various stakeholders in advance. Don't just talk to the senior people. You need to connect with every level to demonstrate you've covered all bases. It's important not to make assumptions. Take the time in advance to engage with several members of the audience by asking probing questions to uncover how they are feeling and what they are thinking in order to gain a better understanding of the current situation from their perspective. This means harnessing your empathy so you can actively listen to what your audience has to say. Remember, hearing is involuntary whereas listening is a skill.

There are, in fact, three levels of listening. Level one, the lowest level, is **superficial listening**, where you are pretending to listen but are, in fact, thinking about something else entirely. This could be because you are too focused on what you want to say next. Level two, which is marginally better than level one, is **selective listening**, when you only hear what you want to hear. Level three is **active listening**, where you harness your EQ to listen live in the moment so you can process exactly what the other person is saying. It takes real effort and concentration, and it involves reading their body language and tone of voice – after all, as I explained in Part One, only 7% of communication comes from the spoken word.

By actively listening to your audience in this way, you will gain a really good insight as to what you need to prepare so you can inspire them emotionally and perhaps commercially (if that is appropriate). A great technique to help you achieve this is to understand your audience's personality types using the DISC model, shown below. DISC, first outlined by the psychologist Dr William Marston in his book *Emotions of Normal People*, breaks down personality into four different types: dominant and driven (D), influencing and persuading (I), secure and steady (S), and compliant and considered (C).[11]

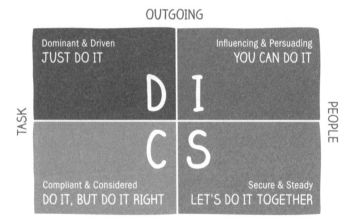

OUTGOING

Dominant & Driven
JUST DO IT

Influencing & Persuading
YOU CAN DO IT

D I

TASK

C S

PEOPLE

Compliant & Considered
DO IT, BUT DO IT RIGHT

Secure & Steady
LET'S DO IT TOGETHER

RESERVED

(Dr William Marston, 1929)

When you look at the diagram, it's important to remember that people are predictably different. Everyone will fall somewhere along the axes of outgoing to reserved and task orientated to people focused. Outgoing types are fast-paced and get their energy from others, whereas reserved types are more measured and self-sufficient. People with a task preference will crave processes and plans, whereas those with a people preference will seek relationships and sharing. Let's now look at each personality type in more detail:

- **'D' STYLE – DOMINANT AND DRIVEN.** Think of people who communicate in a demanding and direct manner. They're motivated by power and compelled to win and get results. For a person who is decisive and determined, their goal is to be in control and their most typical way to communicate is to tell others what to do

- **'I' STYLE – INFLUENCING AND PERSUADING.** These people are interactive and inspirational. They are motivated by praise and recognition. They're eager to get the job done, but unlike the hyper-focused Ds they will want to have fun in the process. Their most likely communication style is to try to influence the other person

- **'S' STYLE – SECURE AND STEADY.** These people are stable and supportive. They like to keep themselves on an even keel and make sure everyone is happy. Their preference is to organize everything as they don't like conflict and want to preserve the status quo. As people who always put others first, their most likely communication style is to listen. They don't want to upset the apple cart with a disruptively strong opinion

- **'C' STYLE – COMPLIANT AND CONSIDERED.** Picture people you know who are motivated by processes and procedures. They need to have a system in place and will be keen to point out what the rules are. Because they are conscientious and detailed, quality is very important to them. Their preference is to communicate in writing, as this allows them to take their time and be accurate and precise

A great way to help you fully understand how these descriptions translate into different personality types is to imagine being in an elevator with a group of people. 'D' types will make a determined entrance, purposefully hitting the 'close the doors' button, while 'I' types won't be able to resist making conversation with the other people. 'S' types will be patiently holding the door open, saying there's plenty of room for more, and the 'C' types will be calculating the weight of everyone in the elevator to make sure it doesn't exceed the maximum capacity!

By recognizing your audience's personality type – and they'll usually be a blend of these types – you will become more informed about how they make decisions, which will give you valuable clues as to the best way to present to them. So, from your first interaction with them, try to notice whether they are more outgoing or reserved. Was their first contact via email or did they pick up the phone to talk to you in person? It's generally easier to spot an outgoing person, so if you can't seem to read them the likelihood is that they tend to be private and therefore reserved.

You need to bear all of this in mind when you ask specific members of your audience questions in advance of your presentation. For example, when you are listening to the needs of a 'D' style personality type, take care to consider that they are likely to be direct and to the point. As such, you need to highlight the impact of the current situation on their results. When you are listening to an 'I' style personality type, ensure you give them plenty of time to talk and air their views. Try to keep the conversation centred on the big picture and avoid focusing too much on the detail. Don't be surprised if you first need to offer your opinion to help the 'S' style personality type feel comfortable enough to open up and share their point of view. If you want to understand the perspective of a 'C' style personality type, you would be wise to ask them in advance so they have time to think about their view and communicate it to you with accuracy.

Now that you are armed with this information, together with your key insights, you can draw on it to put your key messages together in a way that is likely to make your audience feel valued and appreciated. This will make it easier to land your key points, make a genuine connection and build trust. The more effort you put into understanding your audience's needs and matching them with your personal goals, the greater impact you will make. We will talk more about this in Part Four.

3. MANAGING YOUR PRESENTING ENVIRONMENT

Whenever possible, try to become familiar with your presenting environment as this will boost your confidence and make you more comfortable when you actually deliver your presentation. You need to eliminate as many distractions as possible, so that you can set yourself up for success by making sure you are truly present in the moment. These distractions can be physical or they may be emotional (as mentioned in Part One), and both can prevent you from delivering your best performance.

Your aim is to control as much of your environment as possible. Physically, this could mean making sure you turn your phone to silent mode, so you don't get put off your stride, or choosing an appropriate venue for your team meeting (not a noisy café). Emotionally, this could mean making sure you have eaten so you can concentrate properly or are wearing the right clothes so you can walk the talk. It's about managing and mitigating any possible disruptions, so you are able to present the best version of yourself.

A useful tool to help you understand how to manage your environment effectively is the three circles of influence, shown on the next page.

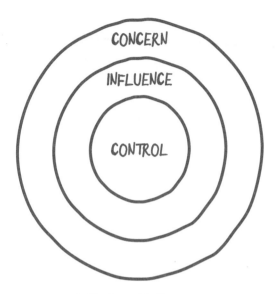

3 Circles of Influence
Adapted From Stephen Covey's book
Seven Habits of Highly Effective People (1989)

The **inner circle** represents the things that are completely within your control, such as the preparation you do, the words you speak and the clothes you wear. The **middle circle** is your area of influence – those things that you can still do something about, such as the use of technology or the choice of venue. The **outer circle** is your area of concern, touching on things over which you have no control – examples could be technology failure or disruptive external noise. These are the things that you can agonize over but ultimately are powerless to change. The secret to effectively managing your environment is to consciously focus your attention on the things within the circles of control and influence, rather than wasting your energy on matters outside your control.

Let's use the scenarios described previously to illustrate how considering your environment in this way can set you up for presenting success. In the case of the department update at the town hall, best practice would be to go to the venue before the presentation to familiarize yourself with the layout. This way, you can work out the best place to stand, decide whether you will use a lectern and wear a microphone, and find out whether there's a place to put a glass of water. These may sound like insignificant activities, but it's amazing how not carrying them out can derail you before your presentation by creating unnecessary interference. By familiarizing yourself with your environment ahead of the presentation, you will have more bandwidth to deliver your key messages live in the moment.

4. PRESENTING IN A VIRTUAL ENVIRONMENT

All too often, people go the extra mile when they are presenting in person or at an external event to an audience they don't know well, but fail to do the same due diligence when they are presenting virtually at a more informal situation to a better-known audience. So, whenever you present virtually, such as on a video call to a member of your team, make sure you focus on your circles of control and influence, and take steps to always appear professional – for instance, don't just wear your gym gear because you are working from home. Think about what can be seen behind you on your video call – is it consistent with the personal brand you are trying to communicate? Clear any empty plates and cups from your desk and check the lighting and angle of the camera – you want the other person to be able to see your face and read your body language properly so you can create a great impression.

It is undoubtedly more challenging to build chemistry when you are presenting in a virtual environment than it is when you present in person. Therefore, you need to dial up your energy so you can amplify your body language and communicate with confidence. You need to set yourself up for success by showing your face as much as possible when you are online. If you are a more introverted personality type, it can be tempting to hide behind your screen and share your slides instead. I'm sure all of us have been on webinars where all we saw was the presentation deck. So, be brave and make eye contact with your audience. Use your knowledge of their personality types to help you build a meaningful connection. As a rule of thumb, less really is more when it comes to presenting online. Keep your slides simple and try to avoid speaking for more than six minutes without asking your audience a question to keep them engaged in what you have to say. This is particularly important if you are talking to 'I' style personality types. Make sure you carefully walk your audience through your slides to help keep them on board. 'C' style personalities will appreciate your attention to detail in this respect. However, don't be tempted to rote-learn a script – your aim is to appear human and authentic.

Finally, make sure you are comfortable with the technology you are using to present online. It's important to take practical steps to familiarize yourself with different virtual platforms, whether it's Zoom, Microsoft Teams, Skype or Google Hangout to name but a few, so you can optimize the experience for your audience. For example, if you are presenting to your team, you may want the option to use virtual breakout rooms, or, if you are presenting to a large audience, you could use a poll to ask questions. It can sometimes be difficult to manage the technical aspects of virtual presenting while delivering a presentation, so consider asking a colleague or friend to support you. For example, they could help to answer any questions that appear in the chat box. This can reduce any emotional interference, giving you more headspace to focus on how to deliver your presentation in a way that keeps your audience fully engaged. We'll look at exactly how to do this in the next two parts of this book.

I hope this part has highlighted the importance of preparing for each and every presenting situation, not just those formal high-pressure ones. By identifying the purpose of the situation, understanding the needs of your audience, aligning these needs with your personal goals and managing your environments in the physical and virtual worlds, you will put yourself on the front foot when it comes to delivering your presentation.

KEY TAKEAWAYS

Here's a quick reminder of the main points we've covered to help set you up for presenting success:

- If you fail to plan, you plan to fail – prepare ahead for each and every presenting situation so you can present the best version of yourself
- Don't save your preparation for formal, high-pressure situations – it's just as important to prepare for internal audiences and informal situations
- Start with the end in mind and identify the purpose of the situation – what is the outcome you want to achieve from your situation?
- Use the Think, Feel, Do model to help you understand your audience's mindset – ask yourself what they think, feel and do currently and what you want them to think, feel and do after they have listened to your presentation
- Clarify your audience's needs by using your EQ to ask clever questions and listen with empathy to their response
- There are three levels of listening: superficial, selective and active; you need to actively listen live in the moment so you can process what your audience is thinking and feeling
- Remember to read beyond the words so you can uncover your audience's real needs
- DISC is a powerful technique that can help you to identify your audience's personality types and discover the most effective way to present to them

- DISC breaks down personality into four types: dominant and driven, influencing and persuading, secure and steady, and compliant and considered
- Use the descriptions of the different personality types to help you understand your audience's personality and work out how you can flex your communication style accordingly
- If possible, familiarize yourself with your presenting environment so you can manage and mitigate any disruptions
- These disruptions may be physical interruptions or emotional interference – both of which reduce your ability to manage yourself live in the moment
- Use the three circles of influence to identify those things in your environment you can control and influence, instead of spending your time worrying about those concerns that you can do nothing about
- Prepare for virtual presentations as carefully as you would for in-person formal ones, by dressing appropriately and ensuring the backdrop to your call looks professional
- Show your face online and engage with your audience by asking questions as you walk them through your slides
- When presenting online, amplify your body language and use your knowledge of your audience's personality types to help you build chemistry
- Develop your technical skills so you can maximize what you get out of the different platforms available to you and optimize the experience for your audience

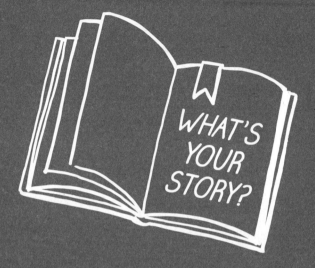

PART FOUR

WHAT'S
YOUR
STORY?

IMPRESSING
YOUR
AUDIENCE

When was the last time you sat through a presentation, surreptitiously checking your watch or phone and wondering just how much longer the person was going to talk for? Perhaps the content of the presentation was vanilla and bland and didn't resonate with you, or maybe the tone of the person presenting was monotonous and dull, or perhaps you just had too much on your mind to be able to focus your time and attention on what the other person was trying to tell you.

Drawing on your empathy and putting yourself in the shoes of your audience is a powerful way to remind you of the importance of capturing and holding their attention. Ask yourself what you tend to think about when you are on the receiving end of a presentation – examples could be wondering what time lunch is or planning how quickly you can get back to your desk so you can crack on with your to-do list. If you are faced with this level of interference in formal presentations, now think about how challenging it is to make a lasting impression in an informal presenting situation where there are even more competing demands for your audience's attention. Experts estimate that we have approximately 70,000 thoughts per day – that's an average of 2,500 to 3,300 thoughts per hour,[12] which is a lot of potential distractions.

Your overriding aim as a presenter is to use the information you have gathered about your audience's needs to cut through this interference and land your key messages in a way that leaves your audience feeling compelled to listen to you and inspired to do things differently as a result of what you have told them. The graph on the next page highlights the important role confidence plays in impressing your audience and encouraging audience participation.

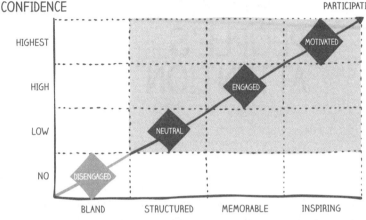

CONFIDENCE

HIGHEST

HIGH

LOW

NO

BLAND STRUCTURED MEMORABLE INSPIRING

PRESENTATION STYLE

As your confidence levels increase, your presentation style progresses from bland to structured to memorable and finally inspiring. At the same time, your audience's mindset shifts from disengaged to neutral to engaged and then motivated. You may focus solely on preparing the content of what you are going to say – in formal presentations, this is usually the presentation slides – rather than how you say it. However, in fact, the secret to becoming an inspirational presenter is to deliver a polished and confident performance. Throughout this part of the book, we'll look at the practical steps you can take to capture and hold people's attention by building a compelling story that inspires your audience and motivates them to do things differently.

1. CAPTURING PEOPLE'S ATTENTION

Let's start with the bad news: people's attention will deteriorate quickly over time. As the graph below shows, the best you can hope for is about 20 minutes. However, if you are talking to senior management, it can be as little as ten minutes before they lose their concentration. The key to stopping this happening in your presentation is to capture your audience's attention by adding spikes of interest through what you are saying, your tone of voice and your body language (we'll cover these last two aspects in the next part of the book).

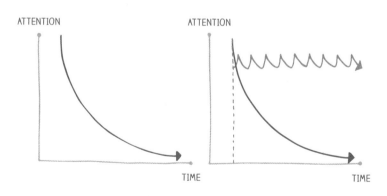

Your audience is most likely to judge whether it's worth their while listening to what you have to say at the beginning of your presentation. This means you need to start with a bang, not a whimper, and make your introduction count so you can hook them in. First and foremost, you need to establish your name and credibility. You'll be amazed how many people start their presentation and forget to say their own name or the name of their company. Don't assume people know your background – instead, tell them why you are an expert in your field, using any qualifications or experience to help you project confidence and credibility without appearing arrogant. In formal presentations, it's likely someone else will introduce you but you still need to grab the audience's attention by articulating the theme of your presentation and why people should listen to you. The same is true if you are presenting to an audience that already knows you; remind them how long you've been working with them or of a recent success you've had. For example, if you are presenting a new product internally, you could start by saying, "Based on the success of last year's launch, I'm here to talk about this season's launch."

Remember, your aim is to focus on fulfilling your audience's needs by showing them what's in it for them. Don't just present from your company's point of view. A powerful way to illustrate this is to compare these two opening statements: "I'm here to update you on this year's new product development projects" versus "I'm going to update you on our new product development pipeline and how this will help you reach your growth targets." The second one clearly articulates the benefits to your audience of listening to what you have to say and is therefore more likely to engage them.

When you introduce your presentation, resist the temptation to dive straight into the detail. Instead, aim to create a memorable opener that captures your audience's attention. Below are some tried-and-tested techniques to help you hook your audience in:

- Use the insights you've identified before to engage your audience
- Start with a rhetorical question that strikes a chord with your audience, such as "How exactly will we meet our budget?"
- Discuss a current event or anecdote that is topical and relevant
- Make a provocative statement or share an impressive statistic
- Use humour to break the ice but only if it seems natural and not forced

A powerful way to see these techniques in action is to go online and watch some of the most popular TED Talks. If you haven't already seen it, I suggest starting with the most watched TED Talk of all time, Sir Ken Robinson's entertaining yet deeply moving talk "Do Schools Kill Creativity?"[13] With more than 65 million views to date, Robinson immediately captures his audience's attention with his self-deprecating humour. He then proceeds to tell an amusing anecdote about a dinner party to make a connection with his audience, build rapport and introduce his theme of education. The use of a rhetorical question draws us in – in fact, the very title of his talk is thought provoking. Robinson uses emotive language such as 'kill' to engage and challenge his audience to consider the real role of education. Now, I'm not suggesting you use humour as a way of introducing yourself if you know you really aren't funny – it's about drawing inspiration from great presenters and then introducing your presentation in an authentic and confident manner.

The final step in creating a strong introduction is to set up the ground rules for your presentation. By ground rules, I mean how you want the audience to behave and interact throughout your presentation. For example, do you want them to ask questions as you go along or would you prefer to have a Q&A session at the end? This is important as the former option gives your audience permission to take control and interrupt your flow – therefore, you need to have strategies in place to manage these interruptions. Below is a quick reminder of the key things you need to include in a strong introduction.

STRONG INTRODUCTION CHECKLIST

- Establish credibility and project confidence
- Your name and the theme – show experience, not arrogance
- Memorable opener:
  - » Key insights
  - » Rhetorical questions
  - » Statistics, topical quotes
  - » Engage with humour
- Ground rules

2. STRUCTURING A COMPELLING STORY

Now that you have a clear idea about how to capture your audience's attention, you need to structure a compelling story so you can keep them engaged throughout your presentation. In the simplest terms, you need to tell them what you are going to tell them, tell them it and tell them it again. A great way to help you understand how to land your main points is to think about how broadcast newsreaders present information – they start with the headline, then give you the content and finish with a summary. In terms of structuring your story, I suggest breaking it down in the following way:

- Strong introduction (10%)
- Inspiring content (80%)
- Confident end (10%)

The biggest mistake most people make when structuring their story is trying to cover too much ground. When it comes to writing a presentation, less really is more. It has been said that the secret to a great presentation is a good start and a good finish – as close together as possible! So, try to keep it succinct. There's a reason that TED Talks are not allowed to exceed 18 minutes. According to TED Talk's curator Chris Anderson, 18 minutes is concise enough to hold people's attention, succinct enough to be taken seriously and long enough to say something that matters.[14] You therefore need to distil your area of expertise into a digestible format by making the complicated easy. This takes time and effort; as various authors have been credited with saying, "I didn't have time to write a short letter, so I wrote a long one instead."

As I mentioned in the previous part of this book, you need to start with the end in mind – the outcome you want to achieve from your presentation. You then need to set the context, explaining all the reasons why the audience should buy into your idea. Inspirational presenters take their audience on a journey by harnessing the power of storytelling.

Since the creation of language, stories have been at the root of our ability to communicate and understand what is going on in the world around us. Stories capture our attention and engage us in a way that facts and figures never do. And, with research showing that we are 22 times more likely to remember a story than we are a fact,[15] it's not surprising that Rudyard Kipling remarked, "If history were taught in the form of stories, it would never be forgotten."

If we refer again to Sir Ken Robinson's TED Talk, it is clear that he doesn't rely on visuals or slides to convey his main points. Instead he tells his audience compelling stories to reinforce his key message that the educational system needs to be reformed. These include personal stories about his son, amusing stories about William Shakespeare and an inspirational story about the choreographer Gillian Lynne. What all these stories have in common is a theme that articulates the need to cultivate creativity in children and acknowledge multiple types of intelligence.

Now it's your turn to create a compelling story that communicates your main theme. Broadly speaking, there are seven storytelling structures you can use to bring your presentations to life:

1. **OVERCOMING THE MONSTER.** A heart-warming story of bravery where the hero or heroine overcomes evil against all the odds. Use it to demonstrate how you have overcome a particular challenge or obstacle

2. **RAGS TO RICHES.** A coming-of-age tale where the hero or heroine overcomes poverty and hardship to achieve great success and wealth. Use it to explain how you have overcome early struggles by taking risks

3. **VOYAGE AND RETURN.** A story of travelling to new lands and returning wiser and stronger. Use it to show that you are prepared to move out of your comfort zone to learn something new

4. **THE QUEST.** A tale of a group of characters setting off together on a journey to achieve a specific mission or goal. Use it to highlight the important role teamwork plays in realizing new objectives

5. **COMEDY.** A classic tale showing the transition from a state of confusion to one of enlightenment. Use it to show the important role communication plays in avoiding confusion and conflict

6. **TRAGEDY.** A cautionary tale showing the downfall of a villain who chooses the wrong path. Use it to illustrate how you can learn from your mistakes

7. **REBIRTH.** A story of a villain who finds redemption and becomes a better person. Use it to show that change is always possible and that you can make better choices in life

By framing your presentation using one of these story structures, you are more likely to be able to cut through the interference in your audience's heads and take them on a journey with you. However, if you feel your presentation doesn't fit any of these structures, don't try to force it. Whatever your story structure, you now need to bring it to life with specific storytelling techniques that make it stand out and leave a lasting impression.

3. MAKING YOUR STORY MEMORABLE

This is where you include spikes of interest to keep your audience engaged so that they actively listen to what you have to say. You want your audience to remember what you said long after you have finished presenting. If we refer back to the most watched TED Talks, it's clear that they rarely use PowerPoint slides to convey their key messages. The emphasis is on what they say and how they say it. So, don't be tempted to overload your slides. Your PowerPoint deck should complement what you say, not be a crutch. Instead, focus your time and energy on incorporating some of the following techniques into your story:

TEN WAYS TO MAKE YOUR STORY MEMORABLE

1. **USE ANALOGIES.** A great example of this is when Steve Jobs said in an interview in 1990, "A computer is the equivalent of a bicycle for our minds." The use of compelling parallels helps to connect people on an emotional level[16]

2. **ASK RHETORICAL QUESTIONS.** An example would be, "Why is innovation important to business today?" These types of questions are useful tools that prompt the other party to think. They also enable you to introduce and communicate important messages

3. **USE REITERATION.** Repetition is an effective way to secure a key point. Climate activist Greta Thunberg used this to great effect when she challenged the world leaders at the United Nations in 2019, saying, "How dare you, how dare you, how dare you."

4. **SELL THE NUMBERS.** Always present numbers in the best way possible to support your argument. This could mean breaking down large numbers so they seem smaller or making small numbers seem larger. For example, offering a 90-day warranty, as opposed to one lasting three months, seems like a better offer

5. **PAINT A PICTURE.** Add visuals to bring your story to life but remember that they shouldn't replace key data or insight. For example, create mock-up imagery for the new product you're trying to sell, or draft an imagined press release to show the other party what success would look like

6. **REFER TO OTHERS.** Making comparisons to relevant others is an effective way to introduce a different perspective and establish credibility. For example, this could be highlighting similar actions successful competitors have taken

7. **USE PROPS.** Props can be a powerful way to highlight your key message, as Jamie Oliver showed in his TED Talk when he filled a wheelbarrow full of sugar cubes to show the amount of sugar contained in one year's worth of an average student's flavoured drinks[17]

8. **DO SOMETHING UNEXPECTED.** Often actions speak louder than words, as shown when Barack Obama dropped his microphone at his final White House Correspondents' Dinner, saying, "I just have two more words to say: Obama out."[18]

9. **USE MULTIMEDIA.** Videos and music can add variety to your presentation and make the audience sit up in their chairs. But keep the clips short – ideally about 60 seconds, otherwise you risk your audience switching off. Always ensure you adhere to and respect copyright permissions

10. **END WITH CONVICTION.** Stop talking before your audience has stopped listening. Make your final words memorable by recapping the purpose of your presentation, including (when appropriate) your call to action

It's useful here to refer back to the DISC diagram on page 60, as people with different personality types will respond in different ways to these storytelling techniques. For example, a 'D' style personality will have a shorter attention span than most as they want to get on and just do things. They are likely to respond positively to the use of props and multimedia as they can convey your messages clearly and succinctly. 'I' style personalities, on the other hand, are more likely to appreciate your use of analogies and ability to paint a picture. Being people focused, they will be drawn to any personal anecdotes. 'S' style personalities are probably the best listeners of all as they are measured and calm. However, they may not appreciate the unexpected as they are often resistant to change. Finally, 'C' style personalities make decisions based on evidence, so they will remember how you sell the numbers, points that you reiterate and your references to third parties.

Clearly, if you are presenting to a large group of people of different personality types, you need to mix up the techniques you use. However, when you are presenting to individuals or smaller departments, use your knowledge of their personality style to help you include the storytelling techniques that are most likely to make a lasting impression on them.

KEY TAKEAWAYS

I've covered quite a lot of ground in this part, so here's a quick summary of the practical steps you can take to impress your audience:

- Put yourself in the shoes of your audience to understand the best way to capture and hold their attention
- Your aim is to cut through the interference in people's minds so you can land your key messages
- The more confident and memorable your presentation style is, the more inspired your audience will feel
- It is most likely that the attention of the people you are presenting to will deteriorate after 20 minutes, so you have to hook them in from the beginning
- Add spikes of interest to keep your audience engaged in what you have to say
- Create a memorable opener by introducing yourself and establishing your credibility
- Focus your talk on fulfilling your audience's needs by reminding them what's in it for them and why they should listen to what you have to say
- Capture your audience's attention from the beginning using insights, rhetorical questions or humour
- Set the ground rules from the start so that your audience understands how you want them to interact with you
- Harness the power of storytelling to win your audience's hearts and minds
- Take your audience on a journey by creating a compelling story using one of the seven types of story structure

- Make your story memorable using techniques that bring your story to life and help inspire your audience to take action
- Refer back to the DISC diagram (see page 60) and use your knowledge of your audience's personality styles to identify the best ways to leave a lasting impression in their minds

PART FIVE

DELIVERING
WITH
CONFIDENCE

Now that you have put together the content of your formal or informal presentation, it's time to focus on how you go about delivering a confident and polished performance. This is the part that most people dread. So, if you get heart palpitations at the mere thought of going on stage, you're certainly not alone, as shown when comedian Jerry Seinfeld said, "According to most studies, people's number one fear is public speaking. Number two is death. ... This means to the average person, if you go to a funeral, you're better off in the casket than doing the eulogy."[19]

It's generally believed that about 10% of people love public speaking and another 10% are completely terrified of it, which leaves about 80% who experience some degree of anxiety at the thought of speaking in public. It's important to recognize that this anxiety is entirely normal. It's in our DNA. There is an evolutionary basis for why we view pairs of eyes watching us as a potential threat – combine this with the fear of being judged and it's not surprising that public speaking can trigger the 'flight, fight or freeze' response. With adrenaline coursing through our body, we can experience the following physiological symptoms:

- Increased blood pressure
- Increased perspiration
- Dry mouth
- Stiffening of the upper back muscles
- Sweaty palms and shaking hands or legs
- Nausea and a feeling of panic

This can have the effect of catapulting you straight out of your comfort zone and into your panic zone (see Part One). The focus of this part of the book, therefore, is to give you the tools and techniques you need to be able to move into and stay in your stretch zone so you can perform at your best when you are delivering your messages. This means leveraging a key emotional intelligence (EQ) skill – your ambition. It's easy to be average, but it takes ambition and optimism to keep raising the bar so you can make a great impression that stands out from those of your peers. To do this successfully, you need to harness everything you learned in Part One about developing your presenting confidence and apply it to your delivery.

The secret to banishing any nerves and delivering a confident performance is preparation, but it needs to be the right type of preparation. Don't spend ages writing your presentation, only to grab it off the printer and have a quick read through before delivering the presentation itself. Great presenters know their content inside out and have honed their delivery style over time to keep their audience engaged. Remember the communication rule on page 17, which breaks down the power of your message: 7% comes from the words you use, 38% comes from your tone of voice and 55% comes from your body language. However, when it comes to preparing your delivery, you need to adopt a much more balanced approach and spend equal amounts of time practising **what you say**, **how you sound** and **how you appear**.

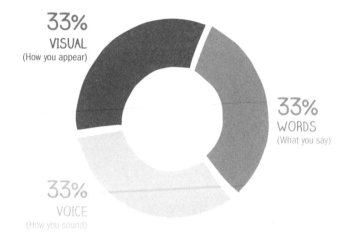

33%
VISUAL
(How you appear)

33%
WORDS
(What you say)

33%
VOICE
(How you sound)

Let's now look at each of these three areas in turn, so you can take practical steps to hone your delivery and boost your performance.

1. FOCUSING ON WHAT YOU SAY

Now that you have created your compelling presentation, you need to focus on the actual words you use to deliver your key messages in order to make the most impact. This doesn't mean you have to memorize each word and know your script off pat – in fact, this can actually undermine your delivery. By focusing on being word perfect, you are less likely to interact with your audience in an authentic manner.

Instead, you need to practise using confident language and avoid what I describe as 'weak speak'. Some examples of weak speak are 'hopefully', 'probably' and 'maybe' – words that undermine your position as a subject matter expert. People often use weak speak because they are thinking out loud and haven't really planned what they are going to say. A great way to eliminate weak speak is to give yourself thinking time live in the moment. So, don't be afraid to pause for thought. Remember, being steady and in control is better than saying the first thing that springs to mind. By working hard at using clear and precise language, you will immediately appear more confident. Removing weak speak will not make you appear arrogant. Rather, you will come across with confidence, and confidence is contagious.

Your ability to communicate clearly and concisely is key to delivering a confident performance. This is particularly important if you are including slides of data in your presentation. I can't tell you the number of times I have seen presenters in boardrooms gesturing to a complex slide packed with facts and figures, only to skim over the content by saying, "As you can see from this slide..." You need to remember that your audience is viewing your slide for the first time and will take a while to digest all of the information on it. So, make it easy for them to understand what you are saying by walking them through each slide in detail. For this to work effectively, you need to make sure your slides aren't too complicated and highlight the key message you are trying to deliver.

For example, the table and chart below illustrate two different ways you can communicate key information and the impact this has on your audience. The table shows two groups of salespeople – one who had received EQ training and one who hadn't – and how this impacted their performance over Quarter 1, Quarter 2 and Quarter 3.

	CONTROL $	EQ TRAINED $	% DIFFERENCE
QUARTER 1	478,105	512,050	+7.1%
QUARTER 2	460,016	530,858	+15.4%
QUARTER 3	466,125	528,586	+13.4%

This table is fairly difficult to interpret from a quick glance. Its key messages are difficult to decipher, particularly if we compare it with the way the same data is depicted on the following page.

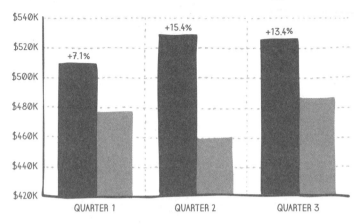

**Salespeople Who Had Received EQ Training
Out-Performed Their Peers by an Average of 12%**

In contrast, this slide more clearly communicates the key message via the headline – i.e. salespeople who have EQ training outperform their peers. The use of a bar chart with different colours would facilitate your audience's ability to quickly understand the data. However, you would still need to talk them through the *x* and *y* axes to explain what they represent. This takes practice.

Make sure you take the time to rehearse and sense-check each slide, and keep honing your words so that you take your audience with you on a journey. Remember, you need to tell them what you are going to tell them, tell them and tell them again. This is not being patronizing – it's helping them to understand exactly what you are saying.

2. FINE-TUNING HOW YOU SAY IT

CLARITY
VOLUME
INFLECTION PITCH DICTION
TONALITY PAUSE PACE
INTONATION
PROJECTION
TONE

In my experience, there is a real difference between how your words sound in your head and how they actually sound out loud. It's often only when you first hear your voice in the live scenario that your nerves start to kick in, so try to pre-empt this by devoting time and effort to preparing *how* you deliver your words in your presentation. Your voice is a powerful weapon that gives your words meaning, interest, purpose, conviction and energy. The exact words you use will have different meanings depending on the way in which you say them. For example, think of the word 'hello.' Depending on the pitch, tone and volume you use, it can have myriad meanings. It can be used as a friendly greeting, to get someone's attention or to find out what's going on.

Throughout your presentation, you need to speak with intention by staying focused on the outcome you want to achieve. For each of your key messages, recognize the objective you want to achieve, then think about *how* you are going to get this across. Consider the powerful effect that tone of voice can have on the meaning of a sentence.

For example, imagine you are communicating the results of your company's staff engagement survey (a type of survey many companies use to assess how focused, engaged and motivated their employees are). If you used a strong tone of voice, listeners might interpret positivity, energy and enthusiasm. The same words said in a hesitant tone of voice might convey disappointment and concern about poor performance. By using a variety of speech devices including intonation, projection, tone and volume, you can add spikes of interest that keep your audience engaged. Nothing is more off-putting or disengaging than a presentation delivered in a monotonous fashion. It can actually be quite distracting for the audience.

A powerful way to liven up your presentation is to focus on the three Ps: pacing, precision and pitch.

Let's start with your **pace**. The optimum pace for presenting is 127 words per minute. To help you understand what this pace of speaking sounds like, dig out a copy of your favourite book and time yourself as you read 127 words of it out loud. Most people, when they are under pressure, either speed up to get their 'ordeal' over and done with, or slow down as they try to remember their 'script'. It may seem like 127 words a minute is slow, but it will give your audience time to understand what you are telling them. You still need to vary the pace – no one likes to listen to a robot, so speed up slightly to show enthusiasm and don't forget to pause if you want to highlight that you have landed a key message.

Now let's focus on your **precision** and the way you enunciate your words. If you have a British accent, I'm not suggesting you need to speak with RP (received pronunciation, also known as BBC English and Standard British pronunciation) like presenters in the 1950s. Everyone has an accent; however, some are harder to understand than others, so take the time to consider your own. You need to ensure that you clearly articulate your words. This is particularly important when you are presenting on a conference call where people can't read your body language or if you are speaking with people from different countries.

I'm probably showing my age now, but a great example of the importance of precision is the classic Two Ronnies comedy sketch in which Ronnie Barker goes into a hardware store asking for "fork handles" but is given "four candles." If you trip over your words, it's easy to give the wrong message. Make sure your diction is clear and precise, so you avoid any confusion.

Finally, remember to vary your **pitch** and volume to keep your audience engaged. If you speak quietly to start with, people are likely to lean in and listen to you. You can then turn up the volume to project your words and land your key messages. The secret is mixing things up so that you keep your presentation interesting and memorable.

3. REMEMBERING TO WALK THE TALK

You should have spent 66% of your time preparing what you say and how you say it, so now it's time to spend the last 33% focusing on how you appear. This is your physical presence and the non-verbal cues you communicate to your audience. It's important to bear in mind that most audiences are friendly and want you to perform to the best of your ability. It's uncomfortable watching someone look nervous or awkward, and it can distract people from listening to what they have to say. So, try to reassure your audience that they are in safe hands by acting and looking the part. Your aim is to own the room, which means walking the talk. Just as it's difficult to say something positive with a frown on your face, it's challenging to communicate confidence if your hands are shaking and you are finding it hard to make eye contact.

The first step is to draw on your self-awareness to help you understand what your body language says about you. It's often useful to ask a friend or colleague for feedback. Be brave and honest about how you appear. Do you have any nervous tics when you present – perhaps you touch your tie or tuck your hair behind your ear when you're feeling under pressure? This is entirely normal, and in some cases it can make you appear human and authentic. It's really only an issue if it is distracting, in which case you need to take steps to try to minimize it.

Imagine a drum roll: you need to feel like this is your moment and you are ready to command the stage. Some people prefer to present to strangers, others to people they know. In either case, actively focus on your body language and make sure you get eye contact with your audience. An insider tip to help you achieve this is to look just above the person's eyes – they will think you are looking directly at them but you are less likely to get distracted. As a rule of thumb, you need to hold eye contact for the length of a thought. Once you've landed your message, there should be a smile or nod to show you have connected with that person and then you can move on. Try to look at as many people as possible and don't just talk to the most important person in the room.

I'm often asked where the best place is to stand for a formal presentation. Generally speaking, you should start by standing with your feet hip-width apart, so you are balanced. You don't want to look like you're swaying on the spot. Your shoulders should be relaxed. Don't put your hands in your pockets as you will need them for gesturing to help you communicate your key points. Depending on your confidence level, you should ideally move around the stage as this creates energy and interest and enables you to interact with different parts of the audience. However, if you feel you need to refer to notes, you may be more comfortable standing at a lectern where you can easily glance down and look at your flashcards while still keeping your hands free to gesture to your audience. Whether you are presenting formally or informally, hand gestures allow you to draw your audience in and create energy. For example, if you are talking about blue-sky thinking, you can point upward – but your gestures need to be proportionate to the size of the setting. The bigger the stage, the more exaggerated the gesture can be – it will make your presentation all the more memorable and engaging.

When it comes to presenting to someone during a meeting, I always recommend the 'BBC position' – bottom in the back of the chair. This will make sure you are sitting upright, which communicates confidence. If you are across a desk from the person you are presenting to, you need to ensure they can see your presentation slides clearly *and* still get eye contact with you as you communicate your key points. Using a pen to point at the screen can help you direct the other person's attention. When you put the pen down, it can act as a cue for them to look at you rather than the screen and this is your opportunity to catch their eye and land your messages. I generally recommend that if you are presenting to more than two people, it's better to stand to give your presentation. You are more likely to make an impact this way.

4. REHEARSING BEFORE YOU PRESENT

Now that you have prepared and fine-tuned your delivery, it's crucial to rehearse your presentation out loud ahead of the performance itself. While you may be happy to prepare your presentation in your head, it's important not to shy away from rehearsing it in front of other people just because it can be uncomfortable asking for and receiving feedback. As any stage performer will testify, it's the hours behind the scenes that make your performance look effortless on stage. The same is true in the world of sport, as Lord Coe high-lighted when he said, "90% of what it takes to be a champion takes place off the track."[20] If we apply this maths in the context of your performance, this means for a 20-minute presentation you need to spend at least 180 minutes rehearsing.

Therefore, my advice is clear: you need to rehearse relentlessly in order to deliver an inspiring performance. This means adopting a rigorous and disciplined approach to rehearsing. Draw up a plan so you can break down your rehearsal into manageable chunks using the table below to help you.

EXERCISE

	✏️	✏️
REHEARSAL DATES, WITH WHOM AND WHERE		
	✏️	✏️
	✏️	✏️
OBJECTIVE(S)		
	✏️	✏️

Start by speaking your words out loud as you rehearse on your own. Give equal emphasis to rehearsing what you say, how you say it and how you sound. Use technology to help you keep honing your delivery style. Record your voice to notice whether you are speaking at the optimum pace, articulating your words, and using tone, volume and pitch to add spikes of interest. Be brave and set up a phone or iPad to video you as you rehearse. It can be toe-curling to film yourself, but it can be an invaluable tool to help you understand what your body language communicates about you. For example, do you need to increase your use of eye contact, move around the stage more or rely less on your notes?

Finally, choose someone to rehearse in front of who will give you honest and open feedback. Draw on your self-reliance and self-control to take on board their feedback and make any appropriate changes. Encourage the other person to ask you challenging questions during the Q&A section as this will allow you to identify whether there are any holes in your presentation. However, don't let their feedback derail you or undermine your presenting confidence. You are your own harshest critic, so be careful who you compare yourself to. It would be great to present like Steve Jobs or Sir Ken Robinson, but unless you are a newsreader or a keynote speaker who travels the world performing on a regular basis, this is unlikely. Instead you need to be appropriately ambitious. This way you will set yourself up for success and deliver your performance in a confident and authentic way.

Now that you understand how to prepare what you say, how you sound and how you appear, it's about putting the theory into practice. While these principles may be easy to apply to formal scenarios, it may be a struggle to think about them ahead of informal situations.

A great opportunity to hone your delivery style informally is to attend networking events. They are the ideal opportunity to use confident and precise language to introduce yourself. You can then practise speaking with intention to demonstrate your passion and energy and develop positive body language to build rapport and establish your credibility.

KEY TAKEAWAYS

Here's a quick recap of the main points I've covered in this part to help you deliver your presentation with confidence:

- Up to 90% of us will experience some degree of anxiety or panic at the thought of speaking in public
- Adrenaline triggers the flight, fight or freeze response, which can cause heart palpitations, increased perspiration and dry mouth
- Preparation can help to control your nerves so that you stay in your stretch zone (rather than your panic zone) and perform at your best
- Adopt a balanced approach to your preparation – focusing equally on what you say, how you say it and how you appear
- Eliminate weak speak from your presentation and instead use confident and concise language to land your key messages
- Walk your audience through your slides, making it easy for them to digest more complicated information by explaining what any charts or graphs represent
- Your voice is a powerful weapon that gives your words meaning, interest, purpose, conviction and energy
- Use a variety of language devices such as intonation, volume and tone to add spikes of interest that keep your audience engaged
- Learn to speak with intention by recognizing the objectives you want to achieve, then think about *how* you are going to get this across
- The optimum speaking pace is 127 words per minute as it helps your audience to understand what you are telling them

- Use precise language to articulate your key messages and avoid confusion
- Vary your pitch and volume to avoid your presentation sounding monotonous
- Use positive body language to help you own the stage and give a polished performance
- Draw on your self-awareness and any videoed rehearsals to understand what your body language says about you so you can minimize any behaviour that could be distracting to your audience
- Regularly seek eye contact with your audience – don't just speak to the most important person in the room
- Stand with your feet hip-width apart so you are well balanced as you start your presentation
- Use hand gestures to draw your audience in and make your presentation memorable
- When you are presenting in a meeting, position yourself so the other person can see your slides *and* still get eye contact with you as you deliver your key messages
- Use networking opportunities to hone what you say, how you say it and how you appear on an informal basis

PART SIX

STAYING IN CONTROL OF YOUR PERFORMANCE

Whether you're presenting on stage to an audience of 100 or at a team meeting to a group of six, you need to draw on your emotional intelligence (EQ) to direct and control your audience in order to make a great impression. It's useful here to refer back to the three core areas that make up EQ to understand the invaluable role these skills play in helping you to stay in control so you can achieve your desired outcome.

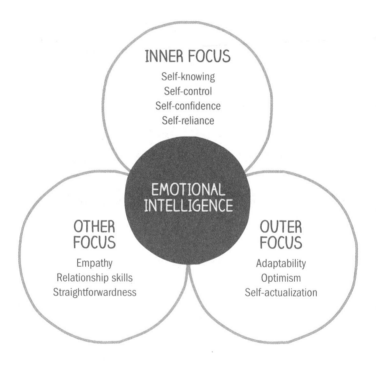

Starting with the EQ skills in the **Inner Focus** circle, you need to harness your self-knowing to read your audience effectively, your self-control to respond rather than react to them, and your self-confidence and self-reliance to back yourself and trust in your ability to own the room and the moment. Moving on to the **Other Focus** circle, you need to draw on your empathy to listen carefully to the questions your audience asks and your straightforwardness to answer them in a way that builds trust and credibility. Finally, looking at the **Outer Focus** circle, your adaptability and optimism are key to thinking on your feet so you can handle your audience's interactions convincingly and feel self-actualized as a result.

In this part of the book, I'll show you exactly how to apply these EQ skills before, during and after your presentation so you can stay in control throughout and keep raising your presenting game.

1. WARMING UP ON THE DAY

First things first: you need to set yourself up for success by remembering to warm up your brain, body and voice on the day of your presentation. Just as athletes wouldn't think about hitting the track without doing a proper warm-up first, you need to draw on your self-control to get your head in the right space before you begin. A powerful tool to help you combat any nerves and adopt a confident mindset is 'visualizing success.' The Olympic swimmer Michael Phelps uses this to great effect as part of his relaxation technique before a competition. He swims each race in his mind before he stands on the starting block so that he is ready for every eventuality. This technique was particularly effective at the Beijing Olympics in 2008, when his goggles filled with water. He went on to win the gold medal in the 200 metre butterfly, despite having to swim the race 'blind,' because he had visualized what he needed to do. So, take a leaf out of Phelps's book and, before you start your presentation, take a few moments to sit down and breathe deeply. Close your eyes and visualize yourself taking your audience through your presentation. Ask yourself – what's the worst that can happen? Then visualize any potential obstacles and how to handle them. This way, if you are thrown any curve-balls in the actual situation, you will already know how to respond to them.

By taking slow, deep breaths and keeping the oxygen flowing, you should feel your body relax. A great way to do this is to breathe in through your nose or mouth keeping your hand on your naval and aiming to feel like you are filling your stomach, before you breathe out fully. Make sure you are properly hydrated but avoid any coffee or caffeinated drinks as this can increase your adrenaline levels. Instead, have a small amount of sugar or glucose or as much as you know your body can tolerate as it can help to wake up your brain. Finally, warm up your voice in the same way that professional singers and actors do. Try humming your favourite song or practising a tongue-twister to help you warm up your vocal cords. This way you will be ready to hit the deck running when you begin your presentation.

EXERCISE

Choose your favourite tongue-twister from the ones below and say it out loud several times before your next presentation.

- Barber baby bubbles and a bumble bee
- David Donald Doo dreamed a dozen doughnuts and a duck-dog, too
- Four fluffy feathers on a fiffer-feffer-feff
- Many mumbling mice are making music in the moonlight
- Nine new neckties and a nightshirt and a nose

2. HANDLING YOURSELF LIVE IN THE MOMENT

Your ability to handle yourself live in the moment depends to a large extent on the amount of preparation you have already done. If you have authored and know the content of your presentation inside out and you have taken the time to rehearse and fine-tune your delivery, you should have the emotional bandwidth to focus on how your audience is responding to you. In other words, you will have minimized the noise or interference in your head, which in turn will allow you to stay in control of your audience and deliver an impressive performance.

As you present, you need to use your eyes and ears to read your audience and determine how engaged they are in your presentation. Watch the room looking for clues – for example, are they smiling and nodding or frowning and looking confused? If it's the latter, don't be afraid to adapt what you are saying to clarify your message. However, remember to judge beyond the obvious. For instance, many people take notes on their phone, so, if you see someone looking at their screen, don't just presume they have tuned out from what you are saying.

You need to harness your empathy to help you manage the mood of your audience. If you sense you are losing their attention, dial up you what you are doing to help keep them engaged. This could mean using a rhetorical question or asking for a show of hands – those spikes of interest that help you to capture attention. Remember, your role is to facilitate your audience's thinking and understanding, and this takes interaction.

Don't be so focused on delivering a good presentation that you forget to actively listen to your audience, otherwise you won't be able to connect with them. Before you give your presentation, you should have decided whether it is more beneficial to take questions as you go along or leave them until the end. Generally speaking, the more formal the presentation, the more likely you are to leave the Q&A to the end, whereas in informal settings it can be easier to answer questions as they arise. However, you need to draw on your awareness and consider the right thing to do for your *particular* audience. Whatever you decide, have the self-reliance to follow through. For example, if people in the audience are interrupting and you've said at the outset that you'll take questions at the end, then politely remind them to hold onto their questions, making sure you remember to come back to them later.

You may dread the Q&A section of your presentation and, in particular, the thought of being asked a question you can't answer. This is the unscripted part where you really do need to be able to listen with empathy and think on your feet. Self-control, adaptability and optimism are key. You need to take the time to respond rather than react to what is being said so you can maintain control of your audience. Below are some practical steps to help you answer challenging questions in a confident and credible way.

HOW TO DIFFUSE DIFFICULT QUESTIONS
- Remember to breathe – this may sound obvious, but it can be tempting to hold your breath when faced with a tricky question, when in fact you need oxygen to help you calm your brain

- Buy yourself more thinking time by giving the person a compliment, such as "That's a really thought-provoking question"
- If the question is outside the scope of what you were discussing, then draw on your inner confidence and say "As you know, I'm here to talk about the launch of our new initiative, so let's focus on the agenda for today" – this will help you keep your presentation on track
- Use your straightforwardness to be honest and open – if you really don't know how to answer a question, come clean and find a credible way to follow up with the individual at a later date; avoid any 'weak speak' and use confident language, saying, "I'm not 100% sure about that, but I will come back to you on that next week" (or whenever is appropriate)
- Use the question to help facilitate discussion by asking the wider audience, "What do you think would happen in that instance?" – this can help you to diffuse a difficult question while boosting audience engagement at the same time
- Rephrase hostile questions in a more positive way to remove the emotion from the situation – by drawing on your optimism instead of being defensive, you will stay in control of your presentation; for example, if the question was in response to statistics about business performance, such as "Don't you think this is an unacceptable performance for a company this size?" you could defuse the situation by saying, "It sounds to me like our company's business performance is really important to you – thank you for raising this issue"
- Control your audience using the mirror principle – your audience will naturally want to copy your emotions and behaviour; this is why, if you are showing any signs of nerves, your audience often feels uncomfortable in response, and the same is true if you show signs of aggression or frustration, such as crossing your arms or shaking your head – it can make your audience become hostile.

The opposite is also true – if you remain cool, calm and collected, and nod and gesture in an open and friendly manner, your audience is likely to copy you and remain engaged in what you have to say

- When it comes to dealing with hostile questions, forewarned really is forearmed – try to anticipate the most difficult questions you are likely to get and then prepare your responses to them

As you take practical steps to direct your audience and keep your presentation on track, you need to follow what I describe as the 'top dog rule.' Ask yourself who is the most important influencer in your audience – it could be a small group of people or an individual – then make it your priority to win their hearts and minds. You need to strike the right balance between focusing on their specific needs and those of your wider audience. However, it's absolutely key that they stay focused on what you have to say. More often than not, once your key influencers are on board with your ideas, the rest of the audience will follow. When it comes to dealing with questions, my advice is to keep the top dog happy first. If you lose their attention, or they have to leave the room to rush off to another meeting, you may have lost the chance for their influence to have the maximum impact.

The secret to making a great impression is to stay in control until the very end of your presentation. Often people are so relieved that their presentation is over and done with that they let it fizzle out or rush off the stage so they can 'be themselves' again. Instead, draw on your self-control to be confident throughout your performance so you can end with conviction. A powerful way to do this is to recap the purpose of your presentation as well as your desired outcome, remind your audience of the benefits of what you are telling them, and reiterate any agreed actions or next steps. Finally, don't forget to thank them for listening to you and encourage your audience to follow up with you in person.

3. REVIEWING YOUR PERFORMANCE

Don't give in to the temptation to tick your presentation off your to-do list and move on without a backward glance. Inspirational presenters adopt a growth mindset and take the time to review their performance so they can make improvements going forward. A great way to assess how you did is to ask yourself what impression you made on your audience. Encourage people in the audience to give you feedback either formally or informally. If your presentation was filmed, make sure you watch it back, then identify what you could start to do differently, what you could stop doing and what you could continue to do. Don't just focus on the delivery aspect of your performance – take into account the preparation and content of your presentation so you can assess the overall impact it has made on your audience.

Additionally, follow up with your key influencers to double check that your messages have landed and that they are taking the right action as a result of what you have presented. If this hasn't happened, you need to draw on your resilience by taking the lessons from the situation and moving forward. Break down your performance into bite-sized chunks so you can identify the specific aspects you need to work on. Then put a plan in place to help you keep raising the bar, whether this means going on a presenting skills course or finding a mentor or coach to boost your self-confidence. By taking a rigorous approach to developing your presenting skills in this way, you will reap the rewards of increased confidence and a greater sense of self-fulfilment.

KEY TAKEAWAYS

The ability to stay in control before, during and after your presentation is key to making a great impression. Here's a quick reminder of exactly how to achieve this:

- Harness all your EQ skills to stay in control and direct your audience so you can keep your presentation on track and achieve your desired outcome
- Warm up your brain, body and voice on the day of the presentation so you can hit the deck running when you begin presenting
- Visualize taking your audience through your presentation, so you can anticipate any obstacles and plan how to respond to them
- Take deep breaths, keep hydrated and avoid caffeine so you can stay in control of your body
- Hum your favourite song and use tongue-twisters to warm up your vocal cords to set yourself up for success
- Use your eyes and ears to read your audience and understand how engaged they are in your presentation
- Draw on your optimism and adaptability to dial up your energy, add spikes of interest and clarify your key messages if you feel you are losing your audience's attention
- Consider the most appropriate time to take questions – for formal presentations this is generally at the end, whereas you may want to be asked questions as you go along in informal situations
- Draw on your self-control and self-reliance to respond rather than react to challenging questions

- Buy yourself thinking time by breathing deeply and complimenting the questioner
- If you are faced with a tricky question, be brave and defer to an expert, ask the audience what they think, or be honest and say you will have to get back to them later
- Rephrase hostile questions into positive ones and diffuse any tension by using warm and friendly body language, which your audience will naturally copy
- Whenever possible, try to anticipate the most challenging questions and prepare your response in advance
- Follow the top dog rule – identify your key influencers and focus your attention on winning their hearts and minds
- End with conviction by recapping your purpose and outcome, reiterating the benefits, agreeing next steps and thanking your audience for taking the time to listen to you
- Adopt a growth mindset: review your performance to identify what you could start doing differently, stop doing and continue to do
- Encourage your audience to give you feedback on all aspects of your presentation, not just your delivery, so you can break your performance down and focus on the specific aspects you need to improve

PART SEVEN

KEEPING FIT FOR PRESENTING SUCCESS

Congratulations on reaching the final part of *The Presenting Book*. By following the practical advice in the previous parts, you should now have a clearer understanding of what it means to harness your emotional intelligence and *do things differently* as you present yourself in formal and informal situations. I'd love to tell you that, just by reading this book, you will always make a great impression going forward. Unfortunately, as any world-class sportsperson or performer will say, it takes blood and sweat to reach the top of your game. So, now comes the hard part: you need to put in the time and effort to practise these presenting skills on a daily basis so you can become a truly inspirational presenter who makes a memorable impression on those around you.

1. PUTTING PRESENTING THEORY INTO PRACTICE

As the saying goes, it takes at least 21 days to develop a habit, so don't procrastinate, adopt a growth mentality and start applying these presenting principles to every interaction you have with people, whether it's on social media, via email, in online meetings, on the phone or in face-to-face meetings. Don't make the mistake of saving your new skills for big, formal presentations. The most lasting way to form a habit is to take simple and easy steps; notice how these steps benefit you and then repeat them as part of your everyday life.

On the next page are some suggestions to help you follow this approach and take your presenting skills to the next level.

TAKE SIMPLE AND EASY STEPS

- Break your presenting goals into manageable chunks by focusing on specific aspects of your presentation – for example, learning to walk the talk or avoiding weak speak
- Use this book as a guide to support you – refer back to the exercises to help you keep on track
- Remember that you don't have to do this by yourself; find a coach, mentor or trusted friend to help you on your journey

UNDERSTAND HOW THESE REWARD YOU

- Recognize that the more effort you put in, the more you will get out
- Track your progress by adopting the principle of 'plan, do, review'
- Put mechanisms in place to reward this behaviour and provide incentives – these could involve congratulating yourself for a job well done when you achieve your desired outcome from a meeting or acknowledging you have had the courage to move into your stretch zone by agreeing to be a speaker on a panel

MAKE IT NORMAL AND EVERYDAY

- Weave the presenting principles in this book into your everyday life
- Make it a habit to prepare before every presentation situation – whether it's formal or informal
- Review your performance after every presenting situation to keep upping your game

It's easy to be average. In my experience, the most successful people in life share the belief that good is not good enough. They aspire to greatness. A powerful way to help you make a great impression is to ask yourself the following four impactful questions before each presenting situation.

WHAT IS MY PERSONAL BRAND?

Refer to your Personal Branding Shield on page 48 to remind yourself how you stand out from the competition, what you want to be known for, what your core values are and what your personal statement is. Remember, you need to behave and communicate these aspects of yourself in a consistent and authentic manner in order to build rapport and credibility. Your goal is to present the best version of yourself each and every time you interact with others.

WHY SHOULD I FEEL CONFIDENT?

Banish any self-doubt and minimize any emotional interference by 'feeding your good wolf' and boosting your inner confidence. Fill in the table on page 28 to remind you why you should feel confident about a particular presenting situation, your relationship with your audience, and your own skills and abilities. Draw on your optimism to reframe any negative thoughts into positives, then find evidence to reinforce this positive thinking so you can embed this new belief.

WHAT ARE THE NEEDS OF MY AUDIENCE?

Prepare ahead by applying the Think, Feel, Do model on page 56 to understand the mindset of the person or people you are presenting to. Then identify what you want them to think, feel and do after you have presented to them. Whenever possible, clarify the needs of your audience by asking clever question and listening with empathy to their response, using the DISC model on page 60 to help you understand their particular communication style.

HOW DO I MAKE A MEMORABLE IMPRESSION?

Capture your audience's attention with a strong introduction and compelling content before ending with conviction. Use the storytelling techniques on pages 85-87 to add spikes of interests to keep your audience engaged. Make your story memorable by focusing on **what you say**, **how you sound** and **how you appear**. Remember, your voice is a powerful instrument that gives your words meaning, interest, purpose, conviction and energy, helping you to create a lasting impression.

2. BUILDING YOUR LEGACY

Whatever stage you are at in your career, it's never too late to make a great impression. Your personal brand will evolve over time as you grow and develop as an individual.

I want to share the story of Alfred Nobel, whose name is today synonymous with peace; however, he originally built his fortune from the destructive power of dynamite. It was only when he read his own obituary in the paper, after he had mistakenly been presumed dead, and saw the headline, "The Tradesman of Death is Dead," that he took matters into his own hands and decided to change his legacy. Horrified that he had been condemned for profiting from the sales of arms and weaponry, he created a fund called the Norwegian Nobel Institute with instructions that the prizes should be distributed to people who had given the greatest benefit to humanity. As a result, to this day, he is remembered as a champion of peace rather than the tradesman of death.

Now, I'm not suggesting that we can all leave lasting legacies of this kind on the world. However, I'm a big believer that there are three types of people in life: those who make things happen, those who watch things happen and those who wonder what happened. By being confident and pledging to present the best version of yourself in all that you do, you will find yourself firmly in the first camp, inspiring those around you and leaving a legacy you can be justly proud of.

KEY TAKEAWAYS

Here's a final reminder of the steps you can take to keep fit for presenting success by putting theory into practice on a daily basis:

- Adopt a growth mindset and weave presenting principles into your daily life, whether via social media, Skype or email, on the phone or in meetings
- Take your presenting skills to the next level by making the process easy, rewarding and normal
- Break your presentation goals down into manageable chunks, using this book and/or a coach or trusted friend to support you on your journey
- Incentivize your progress by giving yourself rewards when you achieve your presenting goals
- Adopt the principle of 'plan, do, review' to measure your progress
- Don't be average – keep raising the bar and aspire to greatness
- Set yourself up for success by asking yourself four impactful questions before each presenting situation:
  » Ask yourself what your personal brand is, so you can communicate consistently and authentically each time you interact with people
  » Ask yourself why you should feel confident – draw on your optimism to flip any negatives into positives so you can feed your 'good wolf'
  » Clarify the needs of your audience so you can understand the most effective way to communicate to them
  » Reflect on how you can make a memorable impression by creating a compelling presentation and fine-tuning your delivery to add spikes of interest that keep your audience engaged

- Remember, it's never too late to make a great impression and change your legacy
- Be confident and pledge to be someone who makes things happen so you can leave a legacy of which to be proud

FURTHER READING

- Anderson, Chris, *TED Talks: The Official TED Guide to Public Speaking,* London: Headline Publishing Group, 2018.
- Babcock, Linda, and Sara Laschever, *Women Don't Ask,* Princeton: Princeton University Press, 2003.
- Bates, Bob, *The Little Book of Big Coaching Models*, Harlow: Pearson Education, 2015.
- Berkun, Scott, *Confessions of a Public Speaker*, Sepastopol CA: O'Reilly Media, 2010.
- Blanchard, Ken, and Don Shula, *The Little Book of Coaching,* London: Harper Collins, 2002.
- Brown, Brené, *The Gifts of Imperfection,* Minnesota: Hazelden Publishing, 2010.
- Bruner, Jerome, *Actual Minds, Possible Worlds*, Cambridge Mss: Harvard University Press, 1986.
- Bungay Stanier, Michael, *The Coaching Habit*, Toronto: Box of Crayons Press, 2016.
- Carnegie, Dale, *How to Win Friends and Influence People*, London: Vermilion, 2006.
- Coe, Sebastian, *The Winning Mind, What it Takes to Become a True Champion*, Chatham: Headline Publishing Group, 2009.
- Covey, Stephen, *7 Habits of Highly Effective People*, New York: Simon & Schuster, 2004.
- Dixon, Matthew, and Brent Adamson, *The Challenger Sale*, London: Penguin Books, 2011.
- Drucker, Peter, *The Effective Executive*, Abingdon: Routledge, 2011.
- Dweck, Carol, *Mindset: The New Psychology of Success*, New York: Random House, 2006.

- Gallo, Carmine, *The Presentation Secrets of Steve Jobs*. U.S.A: McGraw Hill, 2009.
- Gallwey, Timothy, *The Inner Game of Tennis*, New York: Random House, 2015.
- Gallwey, Timothy, *The Inner Game of Work*, New York: Random House, 2000.
- Goffee, Robert, and Gareth Jones, *Why Should Anyone be Led by You?* Boston: Harvard Business Review Press, 2015.
- Goleman, Daniel, *Emotional Intelligence: Why it Can Matter More than IQ*, London: Bloomsbury Publishing, 1996.
- Goleman, Daniel, *Working with Emotional Intelligence*, London: Bloomsbury Publishing, 1998.
- Groskop, Viv, *How to Own the Room*, New York: Random House, 2018.
- Huffington, Arianna, *Thrive*, London: Penguin Random House, 2016.
- Johnson, Spencer, *Who Moved My Cheese?* London: Vermilion, 1999.
- Kline, Nancy, *Time to Think: Listening to Ignite the Human Mind*, London: Cassell Ilustrated, 2002.
- Maslow, Abraham, "A Theory of Human Motivation," *Psychological Review*, Vol. 50 No. 4 (1943): pp. 370–396.
- Mehrabian, Albert, *Silent Messages: Implicit Communication of Emotions and Attitude*, Belmont CA: Wadsworth Publishing Co, 1971.
- Neale, Stephen, Lisa Spencer-Arnell and Liz Wilson, *Emotional Intelligence Coaching*, London: Kogan Page Ltd, 2015.
- Newman, Martyn, *Emotional Capitalists: The Ultimate Guide for Developing Emotional Intelligence for Leaders*, London: Roche Martin, 2014.
- Newman, Martyn, *The Mindfulness Book: Practical Ways to Lead a More Mindful Life*, London: LID Publishing , 2016.

- Oliver, Jamie, "Teach every child about food," February 2010, California, TED video, 21:38, accessed 5 June 2020, https://www.ted.com/talks/jamie_oliver_teach_every_child_about_food?language=en.
- Peters, Steve, *The Chimp Paradox*, London: Vermilion, 2012.
- Pink, Daniel, *Drive: The Surprising Truth about What Motivates Us*, Edinburgh: Canongate Books, 2009.
- Sir Ken Robinson, "Do schools kill creativity?" February 2006, California, TED video, 19:12, accessed 5 June 2020, https://www.ted.com/talks/sir_ken_robinson_do_schools_kill_creativity?language=en.
- Sandberg, Sheryl, *Lean In: Women, Work and the Will to Lead*, London: WH Allen, 2015.
- Sinek, Simon, *Start with the Why: How Great Leaders Inspire Everyone to Take Action*, London: Penguin Books, 2011.
- Soames, Nicole, *The Coaching Book: Practical Steps to Becoming a Confident Coach*, London: LID Publishing, 2019.
- Soames, Nicole, *The Influence Book: Practical Steps to Becoming a Strong Influencer*, London: LID Publishing, 2018.
- Soames, Nicole, *The Negotiation Book: Practical Steps to Becoming a Master Negotiator*, London: LID Publishing, 2017.
- Tracy, Brian, *Eat That Frog: 21 Great Ways to Stop Procrastinating and Get More Done in Less Time*, San Francisco: Berrett-Koehler, 2007.
- Wentz, Lisa, *Grace Under Pressure*, London: LID Publishing, 2019.

REFERENCES

1 Dan Robert Anderson, *Corporate Survival: The Critical Importance of Sustainability Risk Management* (Lincoln U.S.A.: iUniverse, 2005) p. 138.

2 Albert Mehrabian, *Silent Messages: Implicit Communication of Emotions and Attitude* (Portland, ME, U.S.A.): Wadsworth Pub Co, 1980).

3 Timothy Gallwey, *The Inner Game of Work* (New York: Random House, 2001).

4 Billy Graham, *The Holy Spirit: Activating God's Power in your Life* (Nashville U.S.A.: Thomas Nelson, 1978).

5 Abraham Maslow, "A Theory of Human Motivation," *Psychological Review*, Vol. 50 No. 4 (1943): pp. 370–396.

6 Janine Willis and Alexander Todorov, "First Impressions: Making Up Your Mind After a 100-ms Exposure to a Face," *Psychological Science* Vol. 17 No. 7 (July 2006): pp. 592–598.

7 "The 25 Most Trusted Brands in America," Morning Consult. Last accessed 5 June 2020, https://morningconsult.com/most-trusted-brands.

8 A survey from The Ponemon Institute showed a 66% drop in trust in Facebook the wake of The Cambridge Analytica revelations.

9 Zig Ziglar, *See You at the Top* (Louisiana U.S.A.: Pelican Books, 1975).

10 Stephen Covey, *The Speed of Trust* (New York: Free Press, 2006).

11 William Marston, *Emotions of Normal People* (Oxford: Routledge, 1928).

12   Nancy Colier, "How to Live Peacefully With Repetitive Negative Thoughts," *Psychology Today*, 8 March 2017, https://www.psychologytoday.com/gb/blog/inviting-monkey-tea/201703/how-live-peacefully-repetitive-negative-thoughts.

13   Sir Ken Robinson, "Do Schools Kill Creativity?" February 2006, California, TED video, 19:12, https://www.ted.com/talks/sir_ken_robinson_do_schools_kill_creativity?language=en.

14   Chris Anderson, *TED Talks: The Official TED Guide to Public Speaking* (London: Headline Publishing Group, 2018).

15   Jerome Bruner, *Actual Minds, Possible Worlds* (Cambridge MSS: Harvard University Press, 1986).

16   "Bicycle of the mind," YouTube video, 1:17, k0rthaj, 11 March 2013, https://www.youtube.com/watch?v=KmuP8gsgWb8. Accessed 5 June 2020

17   Jamie Oliver, "Teach every child about food," February 2010, California, TED video, 21:38, https://www.ted.com/talks/jamie_oliver_teach_every_child_about_food?language=en.

18   "'Obama out': President Barack Obama's hilarious final White House correspondents' dinner speech," YouTube video, 32:37, Global News, 30 April 2016, https://www.youtube.com/watch?v=NxFkEj7KPC0.

19   "Seinfeld on Fear of Public Speaking," YouTube video, 0:21, Andrew Weissmann, 5 June 2014, https://www.youtube.com/watch?v=HayyRgpO4_I.

20   Sebastian Coe, *The Winning Mind, What it Takes to Become a True Champion* (Chatham: Headline Publishing Group, 2009).

ACKNOWLEDGEMENTS

First and foremost, I want to thank my fantastic family. My mum and dad for being inspirational role models who showed me what it means to make a great impression and own the room. My husband James and daughters Talya and Amelie. I really couldn't do all that I do without your love and encouragement. Thanks to my wonderful team at Diadem, who always go the extra mile and present the best versions of themselves each and every time they deliver training and coaching. Finally, a special mention to Martin Liu and the team at LID Business Media for helping me to share my passion for setting people up for presenting success with an even wider audience.

ABOUT THE AUTHOR

NICOLE SOAMES is a highly qualified coach and emotional intelligence practitioner. She gained extensive commercial experience during her 12 years managing large sales teams at Unilever and United Biscuits, followed by over 15 years developing and delivering training programmes around the world. In 2009, Nicole founded Diadem Performance, a leading commercial skills training and coaching company. With over 100 clients across the globe, Diadem has helped many thousands of people become 'commercial athletes' in influencing, selling, negotiation, account management, marketing, presenting, strategy, coaching, leadership and management.

Nicole's charismatic and energetic communication style and ability to drive change enable people from a diverse range of organizations to think and act outside their comfort zone and unlock their true potential. Nicole is also the author of the bestselling *The Coaching Book*, *The Influence Book* and *The Negotiation Book*, all in the Concise Advice series from LID Business Media. For more information about Nicole's books visit **www.nicolesoamesbooks.com**.

Follow Nicole on Twitter
@NicoleSAuthor.

Get in touch regarding you or your team at
www.diademperformance.com.

FROM THE
SAME AUTHOR

The Negotiation Book
LID Publishing, 2017

The Influence Book
LID Publishing, 2018

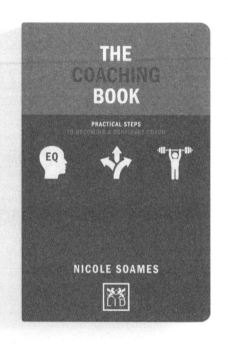

The Coaching Book
LID Publishing, 2019